First published in Great Britain in 1995 by
PAVILION BOOKS LIMITED
26 Upper Ground, London SE1 9PD

A Conrad Goulden Book

This book is typeset in Caslon and Ehrhardt
Designed by Nigel Partridge
Jacket illustrations by Julia Whatley

A CIP catalogue record for this book is available from the
British Library

ISBN 1 85793 675 2

Printed and bound in Great Britain by
Butler & Tanner, Frome

2 4 6 8 10 9 7 5 3 1

This book may be ordered by post direct from the publisher.
Please contact the Marketing Department.
But try your bookshop first.

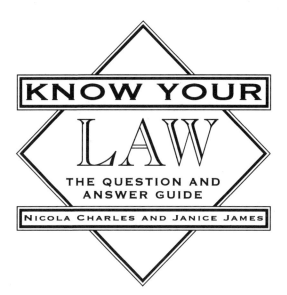

KNOW YOUR
LAW

THE QUESTION AND
ANSWER GUIDE

NICOLA CHARLES AND JANICE JAMES

PAVILION

ACKNOWLEDGEMENT

The authors would like to express their appreciation of the help given by Victor Levene in the compilation of this manuscript.

CONTENTS

AUTHORS' PREFACE

Why did we write this book?

We had already written a guide to the law for women, *The Rights of Woman*. We had had a very good response and many men wrote and asked us why we did not do a general legal book which would help everyone. Some of the material which appeared in our original book is here but we hope now that everyone's questions will be answered within.

As life gets more complex and resort to the law more expensive, we felt there was a real need for a manual which explains clearly and concisely what you can and cannot do about any situation you might find yourself in.

This is not a book which presupposes any legal knowledge. It is not a text book for aspiring lawyers (though it might serve them for reference!) In easy, at-a-glance, question-and-answer form, it deals with the trivial as well as the titanic problems which might crop up in anyone's life.

Buying a house, getting married or divorced, taking a job, are all major decisions with legal implications. But the nub of this book is that *everything* you do in your daily life has legal implications, from handing over your dry-cleaning to buying a train ticket, from ordering a meal in a restaurant to having a haircut. If anything goes wrong, the law will be on your side – or against you.

This guide helps you to understand the law and what your rights are. When you find your problem, we hope our advice gives you the confidence and information to cope with it. With more serious problems, we will set you on the right road, telling you when to seek professional advice and, equally importantly, when you would be wasting your time and money.

If you do not find your problem in the chapter you would expect to, or amongst the cross-referenced questions, turn to the Index at the back where subjects are cross-referenced to help you and, hopefully, we will have covered it elsewhere in the book.

Where possible, we have indicated how the law may differ in Scotland.

While every care has been taken to ensure that the information given is correct at time of going to press, neither the authors nor the publishers warrant the accuracy thereof.

NICOLA CHARLES AND JANICE JAMES

CHAPTER ONE

LOVE, MARRIAGE – AND DIVORCE

When love is in the air and you're walking on it, it's unthinkable that you should ever not agree on everything, so people tend not to make plans for this eventuality. However, it's sensible to come down to earth long enough to plan your future together (or apart). What are your attitudes to children? How will you organize your finances? Shouldn't you make your wills? How will you allot property and belongings? Who will get custody of any children in the event of a divorce?

And if you think marriage is just 'a piece of paper' which you and your beloved don't need, do make sure you have other pieces of paper which state and will safeguard your interests in the event of your relationship breaking up.

———

Q Our daughter wanted a June wedding with all the 'trimmings', including a white Rolls-Royce which was ordered and paid for. On the day, a blue Cortina turned up, the excuse being that the Rolls had broken down. My daughter did go to church in the car sent but she was so disappointed, which in turn upset her mother and me. The car firm has refused any refund, saying that they fulfilled their contract by sending a car and getting the bride to the church on time.

A Ah, but their contract was not to send any old car but a sparkling white 'Roller'. This they failed to do and, in our view, not only are you entitled to the difference in value between what you paid for and what you got, but you should also receive compensation for the disappointment of your daughter and yourselves by what was quite clearly a breach of their contract.

———

Q My fiancée has just broken off our engagement. I really stretched myself to buy her the best engagement ring I could afford. Now she says that she's entitled to keep it and has no intention of giving it back to me. Can she do this?

A If you had broken off the engagement, we would have said that the ring was some sort of compensation for her hurt feelings. Since your fiancée has caused the split, we can only say how disgusted we are that she has not automatically returned your ring. We feel she has a *moral* obligation to do so. Sadly, she does not have a *legal* one. If the ring were a family heirloom, you might be able to make a case in law for its return to the family assets but in your case, the only thing we can suggest is that you send a lawyer's letter asking for its return or, if it was very expensive, take advice as to whether it might be regarded as an investment you had made on behalf of your future relationship.

———

Q Our son is desperately upset. He has lived with his girlfriend for over three years and she is now pregnant. He desperately wants her to have the child and is both willing and happy to marry her. However, his girlfriend neither wants marriage nor the child and is apparently arranging an abortion. Is there anything he can do to stop this?

A No, there isn't. Even if the couple were married, there is nothing that can be done legally to force an unwilling woman to go through with a pregnancy. The only consolation for your son is that it is better that he finds out now how different his views are on having a family from those of his girlfriend. (See also pp. 167, 168.)

———

Q The man next door is a Muslim and has two wives. Supposing I were to 'marry' a second woman, would I still be arrested for bigamy? And if I, an Englishman, became a Muslim, would I be able legally to have more than one wife in this country?

A The man next door must have acquired his wives when he was domiciled in a country where polygamy is allowed – not in England; otherwise he would have committed bigamy – as you would if you marry and then go through another marriage ceremony whilst your first wife is still legally bound to you. In Britain the law of marriage is governed by domicile not religion and whatever religious rules may allow, the law of the land says one wife only for a man who resides permanently in Britain and wishes to marry.

We would have thought that our advice is surely a relief to you: most people feel that one spouse at a time is quite enough, thank you. And remember – if you have two wives, you also have two mothers-in-law!

———

Q My boyfriend split up with his wife six months ago. He is Muslim and he has asked me to marry him under Islamic law in a mosque to purify our relationship. Would this be seen as bigamy under English law? He has not divorced his wife.

A You can happily go and be 'purified' with impunity! Such a ceremony would not be recognized as a marriage under English law and thus no question of bigamy arises. The other side of this, however, is that you gain no rights under the law and could make no claim as a 'wife' if your Muslim 'marriage' ended. Remember that, under Islamic law, all your husband has to do is pronounce 'I divorce you' three times and it's done!

———

Q My daughter is divorcing and she would like to revert to her maiden name. Can you tell us what procedures have to be undertaken and the costs involved? How does she let people know?

A It is through custom not law that most women adopt their husband's surname on marriage. To revert to the use of a maiden name, all your daughter needs to do is inform interested parties (banks, credit card companies, etc.) and then just call herself by whatever surname she chooses. (See also pp. 68, 69, 70, 213.)

———

Q I spent my childhood in a home and then with foster parents. I'm now twenty-four and, after six years' search,

I've been reunited with my long-lost brother. We're so happy. We're also in love as well as loving each other and have set up home together. For obvious reasons, we've decided not to have children. What, however, would be the situation if anyone reported us? Everyone round here accepts us as a married couple.

A We're glad you're being sensible about children. Any genetic defect or hereditary disease would, of course, be more likely to occur in a child born of an incestuous relationship.

This is such a sad situation and not an uncommon one. After your unhappy early years, it is natural that you and your brother should cling to each other and try to make up for lost time.

Technically, you are both breaking the law because a sexual relationship between a brother and sister amounts to unlawful incest. However, the police and the courts deal with incest in accordance with the parties involved. At one end of the scale, where small children are sexually interfered with by adult close relatives, a very serious view is taken – and rightly. Where two adults are concerned, however, as long as there is no element of coercion from either, it is unlikely that any action would be taken against you. (See also p. 19.)

Q I've just discovered that the man I married six years ago is a bigamist. He has a wife and two sons at the other end of the country. Apart from being distraught on my own account, I'm desperately worried about our five-year-old daughter. Does this mean she is illegitimate? And, if so, what would her position be if my 'husband' dies? Would she be entitled to a claim on his estate if he died intestate?

A You haven't said whether you were the first 'wife' in time. If you were then, clearly, you and your children have all the normal rights and benefits arising out of marriage. However, if you went through a wedding ceremony when a wife was already in existence, then your entire marriage was non-existent from the start. However, you are not in the position of a live-in lover because, although the law says you are not and have never been a wife, you are entitled to claim maintenance for yourself and your daughter as if your marriage were valid. As to your daughter, she is treated in just the same way as any other child of her father. There is no longer any distinction between legitimate and illegitimate children for the purpose of inheritance. (See also p. 84.)

———

Q My marriage is very unhappy. We have very little money, which doesn't help, and my husband drinks heavily. He forces his sexual attentions on me and I dread the thought of his coming home at night. I'd like to get away but he says he'd follow me and never let me go. My friends says I can accuse him of rape and get a divorce. Is this true? Even if I did, I'd still be afraid of his catching up with me.

A You do not need to accuse your husband of rape to get a divorce since your husband's general behaviour can certainly amount to unreasonable conduct, which can be the basis of a petition. Pending a divorce and even afterwards, you would be entitled to seek the protection of the court if you feared your husband's threats and advances. You do this by obtaining an injunction restraining him from any molestation of you whatsoever. However, if you feel that the protection of the police is really what you need then, on the facts you give, you could report your husband for rape. Most police stations have domestic sections and will assist and advise you in this distressing situation. (See also p. 16.)

––––––

Q I would like to know whether my husband has the right to half the value of our house when he has paid only towards the mortgage and nothing else. We are now separated, the house has been sold and I have been rehoused by the council because I am disabled. All I have to live on is a small income from an investment I made with money from a previous divorce settlement. My husband, on the other hand, has his own business and has not maintained either me or our two children, who were still at school when we parted.

A If the house was in joint names, your husband could well be entitled to receive his half share of the property. But if your case comes before the court after a divorce, the result depends, in the long run, on the needs and assets of each party. The fact that your husband has never maintained you will be an important consideration when dealing with the distribution of the property. (See also pp. 8, 10, 49, 50.)

––––––

Q Following my divorce settlement, I agreed to buy out my ex-husband's share in our house. I had six months to find the capital, which I did eventually although delays meant that I was three months over the time limit before my ex-husband was paid. He has responded by deducting maintenance payments due to our son for those three months, claiming that he has lost the equivalent interest on the money that was due to him for that period. Can and should I claim the money back from him? I receive no maintenance for myself.

A Your ex-husband had no right to deduct maintenance due to your son and if you were to claim it back, the court would undoubtedly enforce the full maintenance against him. However, if you bring proceedings for this, you do risk facing a claim from your husband for the interest to which he might well be found entitled and you could find that your gain on the one hand is offset by your loss on the other. Whether your claim is a worthwhile exercise depends upon whether your ex-husband were to bring his cross-claim and his mean and small-minded conduct to date makes this likely. (See also p. 17.)

Q My fiancé and I are to be married next year. We have decided to record the occasion on a video. We asked permisson of the deaconess to bring the video recorder into the church. She agreed but informed us that the organist is likely to charge performing rights. Can he do this as no one else has ever heard of it?

A By recording your ceremony, which will include the performance of the organist, he is able to make a charge which relates, not to his playing at your wedding, but for the granting to you of rights to replay his performance when you show the video on later occasions.

Q I was widowed and remarried but my second marriage has ended in divorce. My ex-husband is claiming a share of the property which had been bought by my first husband and left to me in his will. Unfortunately, there was a small mortgage outstanding when I remarried and this was paid by my ex-husband in a lump sum after the wedding. He insisted that I signed a document acknowledging receipt of the payment as a loan to be repaid to him. The property, which is in my name alone, has leaped in value and he now claims an entitlement to at least half. Where do I stand? Our marriage was a disastrous mistake and lasted only four years.

A We must stress that the court has complete discretion to deal with any property as it thinks fit following the breakdown of a marriage. However, in view of the length of your marriage and the facts regarding the purchase and title of the house, we believe it is unlikely that your ex-husband will do as well as he hopes. It may be that because he insisted upon paying off the mortgage as a loan, the court will hold that he is only entitled to repayment of this money plus some interest and this sum is likely to be far less than a percentage interest in your house. In the end, all factors will be taken into account regarding your respective needs, obligations and assets before the final award, if any, is made on his application. (See also pp. 8, 10, 49, 50.)

———

Q My father is in the process of getting a divorce from his wife (not my mother). He was married to her for just under two years when she left him to live with another man. Whilst my father was away for a few days, she returned to his house and removed as many of the household possessions as she could to furnish her new home. She also removed some of my father's personal possessions. Surely she is not entitled to these items as my father owned most of them before he met her?

A If your father is in the process of getting a divorce, there is a procedure under the Matrimonial Causes Act where he can obtain an injunction against his wife for the return of his property. We would advise him to seek this injunction without delay as, clearly, she is not entitled to his personal possessions and it may well be that she is not entitled to a substantial amount of the household possessions which she has also taken. In Scotland, he should pursue an action for delivery. (See also p. 104.)

Q When my husband and I separated, we put some of our possessions in storage. Unbeknown to me, my husband removed a carpet of mine which I had bought before our marriage and subsequently sold it. He now refuses to pay me the £400 that the carpet was approximately worth. Can I sue him for theft and how do I stand legally?

A On the facts of your letter, you can indeed sue your husband for theft – which in a civil action has the technical name of 'conversion'. Your husband has 'converted' your property into cash and you are now able to claim against him for its value. (See also p. 104.)

Q My mother, who is sixty-one, is unhappily married. My stepfather keeps her short of money, is antisocial and pays no attention to her or to the home which they own jointly. My mother has to work in order to keep herself but her health is beginning to suffer. She would like a divorce but is worried that, because my stepfather is seventy-three, she would get nothing from the house if she left him.

A Since the house is jointly owned, your mother has a legal entitlement to half its value. The court has wide powers to deal with property upon the breakdown of marriage and the difference in ages between the parties will not necessarily cause the court to interfere with the legal rights of the parties. It may be a factor to be taken into account, but it will be just one of many considerations when all the needs and assets of the parties are looked at. (See also pp. 7, 8, 49, 50.)

———

Q After I divorced my first husband, he agreed I should have a house for me and our two children. We arranged to buy a property, which is now the subject of argument. The house was bought in his name to ensure that a mortgage could be granted and he lent me half the deposit. Until my new man came on the scene, he also paid the mortgage instalments but that was instead of maintaining the children. My new man has taken over all the outgoings on the house but my ex-husband is now threatening to claim for his share of the value of the property and force a sale of the house. We are very worried by this.

A It is hardly surprising that you are worried by these threats and you must take immediate steps to prevent him selling without your knowledge. A solicitor will be able to deal with this through the local land registry. From what you have said, it does not look like your ex-husband would have any claim to the property – only to the return of his loan of part of the deposit money. Since the house was bought after divorce, then the law would look at what was intended at the time of the purchase to decide whose house it is. It seems that the house was intended for you and you should now take steps to have it transferred from your ex-husband's name – a fairly complex procedure for which you would be well advised to seek help from a competent solicitor. By the way, you can also claim maintenance for the children if you wish through the Child Support Agency. In Scotland, the situation is quite different and the advice of a solicitor is essential. (See also pp. 7, 8, 49, 50.)

————

Q I bought my flat a year before I married six years ago. Because we spent most of our married life overseas, my husband and I lived there together for a total of only seven months. We separated eighteen months ago and he took almost all our joint possessions because he was 'letting me keep the flat'. The mortgage is in my name only and he paid just a few hundred pounds towards the outgoings on the flat during the time we were married. My husband is now making a claim on half of the flat on the grounds that it was the 'matrimonial home'. I'm worried because I have heard that a man is entitled to two-thirds of all joint possessions when a couple without children splits up. When my husband left, he had more than £15,000 of his own in his bank account from the sale of the house that he owned before we were married. Can he really be awarded half of the value of my flat?

A The court has absolute discretion to make orders dividing up property between husband and wife as it thinks fit. There is no set formula to decide who gets what so you can forget what you have heard. This old two-thirds/one-third rule was created by the courts as nothing more than a rough and ready guideline in a limited number of cases. From what you have told us, it would seem most unlikely that your husband would be entitled to any share in your flat. Indeed, he could find himself at the wrong end of your claim against the joint possessions that he helped himself to, particularly if you live in Scotland, where there is a presumption that you are entitled to an equal share of these against his total assets if these are sufficiently large. You must seek expert legal advice, come what may. (See also pp. 7, 8, 49, 50.)

Q I'm sixteen and my boyfriend is seventeen and we're very much in love. We want to get married but our parents won't give their permission. So what we want to know is: can we get married at Gretna Green? If we can, what are the rules: how long do we have to be in residence and could our parents stop the wedding? Also, would the marriage be valid in England?

A Well, our immediate reaction is that you should wait and get married with both your families giving their blessings. Parents do know a thing or two about marriage, you know. However, if you are determined to go through with it, this is the situation: as you are both minors, that is, under eighteen, your parents' consent is required to marry in England and Wales. As you are both over sixteen, you do not require consent to marry in Scotland (Gretna Green being the first stopping post in Scotland over the English border). However, only in cases of exceptional urgency will a Sheriff's licence be issued which dispenses with the usual requirement of the proclamation of banns. Otherwise, you have to make a joint application for the licence and at least one of you must have lived in Scotland for fifteen days before the application is made. If you do go ahead with your marriage at Gretna Green, it will be valid and recognized in England but we stress you should think long and hard before taking such a serious step.

Q My son had an illness when he was a child which the doctors said could make him sterile. When his girlfriend told him she was pregnant and the child was his, he accepted it and married her. This marriage ended in divorce and he has now met another girl he wants to marry. My question is whether he will still be liable to pay maintenance for the child of the first marriage if he now finds out that he cannot have children after all?

A If, when your son married and the child was born, your son, believing his girlfriend, treated the child as his own, he became legally liable for the child whether in fact he was the father or not. Even if he were to discover now that he is and has always been unable to have children, he could not walk away from maintenance obligations which he has towards what the law describes as a 'child of the family'. (See also pp. 106, 107.)

Q My wife and I are separated and planning to divorce. Our marriage was based on a strong sexual attraction on both sides. I have moved out of the family home but we meet to arrange details of who is to have what. She has become very difficult and demanding; not only does she want more than half the proceeds of the sale of the house but she is also laying claim to some furniture which has been handed down in my family for generations. I must admit that on several occasions when we have met, we have made love. This happened again last time and, to my horror, she says she is going to the police to accuse me of rape unless I give way to her financial demands. I'm sick with worry. I've never forced my attentions on her or any woman. She is being vindictive to get what she wants and I just don't know what to do. I'd call her bluff but I think she's quite capable of going through with her accusations. She's always rather enjoyed the limelight.

14

A Your situation highlights precisely the dangers of a 'rape within marriage' or 'date rape' law which, whilst full of good intentions, is fraught with possible problems – including abuse by an aggrieved wife.

Call her bluff – unpleasant for you though it is, we would advise no one to give in lightly to any form of blackmail. In view of the background details, we consider it unlikely that the police would be enthusiastic about bringing charges once they had interviewed you and learned the true position. Obviously, you would be taking a chance but sometimes in life one has to stand up and be counted.

———

Q My husband lost his job some months ago. He has always had a hot temper but it's worse than ever now and he has recently been very violent towards me. I'm at my wits end and scared stiff that I or the children will come to real harm. I can't leave – I have nowhere to go and I don't really want a divorce.

A This is one of the sad, knock-on effects of unemployment. We sympathize with your husband who is, obviously, under great strain. You must, however, seek help. Laws exist to put restraints upon your husband's behaviour by way of court order which, if he disobeys, could land him in prison. The court can even order *him* out of the house if this is considered desirable or necessary for the family's health or safety. You should get advice from a solicitor experienced in domestic matters. You don't need to start divorce proceedings or even be married to get assistance. If you do not want to resort to law, it might be an idea for you to consult a marriage counsellor.

———

Q I had an arranged marriage which was a disaster. I left my husband and now I have met a man whom I want to marry. I am expecting his child soon. My husband will not agree to a divorce. He claims to be the father of my child and says I can never be free of him because of this.

A The only time 'agreement' is required for divorce is where the parties have simply been separated for two years. Divorce is based on 'irretrievable breakdown' and your marriage seems to have well and truly broken down. Your husband's claims to your child cannot prevent a divorce on the appropriate grounds, however reluctant or obstructive he attempts to be. (See also p. 7.)

———

Q My fiancé who is Scottish has voluntarily paid maintenance to his ex-wife who still lives in Scotland. There are no dependent children and she is free and able to work. He also gave her the contents of their council house and £3,000. He agreed to pay her the maintenance, which he could afford at the time. Now he is frequently unemployed and finding it increasingly hard to meet these payments. I have advised him to stop paying as there was no court order. Am I right?

A Without a court order, there is no enforceable agreement and your fiancé can either stop or reduce these payments at any time. However, such an action would be likely to prompt his ex-wife into an application to the court which would then determine the level of maintenance, if any, to be paid, after assessing the needs and assets of both your fiancé and his ex-wife. Your fiancé's ex-wife could apply to a court in Scotland to decide the question of maintenance and any judgment obtained by her can be both registered and enforced by an English court. (See also pp. 7, 18, 66.)

Q I am planning marriage and my fiancé and I have purchased a property upon which we are paying a large mortgage. We were both previously divorced and I have my three children living with us. I receive no maintenance for them as my ex-husband is unemployed. My fiancé has been paying £20 a week maintenance for his daughter under a court order but we are now finding these payments hard to meet in view of our mortgage commitment. My fiancé's ex-wife is also planning marriage. Could we have the maintenance payments reduced? And is it the Child Support Agency that will now determine what he should pay?

A Until 1997 any order for child maintenance made by a court is referred back to the court for any reconsideration of previous orders as long as those orders were made before April 1993. Anything after that date comes under the jurisdiction of the Child Support Agency which applies its own formula to maintenance awards. Assuming your fiancé's order was prior to the operative date, his application will be to the court.

Theoretically, any maintenance payment can be varied by agreement or application to the court. If the ex-wife was unwilling to agree to a reduction, be warned that it is unlikely that the court would reduce the sum since the maintenance is specifically for the child and the ex-wife's change of circumstances would have little bearing on your fiancé's responsibilities towards his daughter. (See also pp. 8, 66.)

Q My husband and I have been married for six years. He had two children from his first marriage and he and I lived together while waiting for his divorce. Only a nominal maintenance order was made for the ex-wife but he paid maintenance for the children and when the sum was decided upon, my income was taken into account. The ex-wife has had regular employment and lives with her boyfriend who also earns good money (although his income was not looked at for maintenance of the children). Now we are planning our own family and I will stop working. Can we have either the maintenance for the children or the nominal five *pence* a year order in favour of the ex-wife stopped? We cannot support two families on one income.

A Since it is likely that the court order was made prior to April 1993 it is to the court that you return and present to them new financial circumstances which might allow for a variation to ease the burden upon the paying party. In respect of the children, maintenance will not be stopped but will be ordered at the maximum amount considered necessary for them and reasonable for your husband to pay taking his reduced income into account. Your own income was taken into account to help assess how much your husband could afford to pay and therefore when you stop working this factor, together with the added responsibilities of a new child, should be put forward to argue a reduction. From what you have said there seems no reason for the court to continue the nominal five pence order for the ex-wife at all. (See also pp. 5, 7, 16, 66.)

Q What is a legal marital relationship? I'm not talking about kinky sex! It's just that my husband died two years ago and I realize that I've fallen in love with his unmarried brother. I have two children from my marriage. My brother-in-law and I would love to get married.

A In the sixteenth century, Henry VIII tried, in vain, to have his marriage to Catherine of Aragon annulled on the grounds that the Church of Rome should not have sanctioned a marriage between a man and his brother's widow. He failed because Catherine's first marriage to Henry's older brother had never been consummated and had not, therefore, been a valid marriage.

Nowadays, the civil law looks more tolerantly at marriage but even so there are prohibitions on certain marriages between classes of relationships.

Most obviously, there cannot be a marriage between siblings (brother and sister) or between 'lineal' relatives whether by blood or adoption (grandparent, parent or child), or even between uncles and nieces or aunts and nephews. Some further restrictions govern marriages between the children of former spouses and the new husband or wife, but you can see that your relationship with your brother-in-law is not within any of these prohibitions or restrictions. You can marry law-fully and we wish you happiness. (See also p. 5.)

CHAPTER TWO

NEIGHBOURS

Soap operas show communities having their ups and downs but, when it comes to the crunch, rallying round and being good neighbours. That's why soaps are so popular – they're not like real life!

Sartre said, 'Hell is other people.' That's often true as our neighbours aren't always as nice as we are. They play loud music, keep nasty dogs, paint their houses orange, block our driveways, chop down ancient trees and build extensions without planning permission.

How can we deal with these minor and major irritations and turn neighbours, if not into friends, at least into people who are reasonably nice to be near?

———

Q Our next door neighbours are making our lives unbearable by being vindictive and spiteful towards me and my family. We had to get rid of our dog because they kept letting him out and complained (falsely) that our dog had damaged their fence. Their son came round and threatened us and we have had visits from the Social Services after 'anonymous' calls that we were abusing our children. It is one thing after another and we wish we could stop them somehow.

A This is not easy for you because complaints about insidious nastiness can be made to sound feeble when pulled to pieces in court proceedings. If, however, you can show that your neighbours' behaviour amounts to harassment, then you might well be able to get a court order against them, especially if you could show that the ghastly son was acting with his parents' knowledge and consent. The threats could, in any event, amount to a criminal offence for which you would be entitled to involve the police. We strongly advise you to take formal legal advice before embarking on any court action in this distressing situation.

———

Q The young couple who live below us have always been a bit noisy: loud music, television and friends in at all hours. We have mentioned it politely and each time they have apologized charmingly. But the disturbance is getting louder and longer each night and is beginning to affect my husband's health. How can we deal with this without falling out with them?

A Sometimes it's easier to cope with nasty people! Charming they may be but you have to grasp the nettle here. A long discussion with your neighbours rather than just a polite 'mention' is necessary. If they are genuinely charming, they will change their ways. If not, you should contact your Environmental Health Department at the local authority who can monitor the noise and deal with the problem on your behalf if they believe this is appropriate.

———

Q I left my flat to move close to my married son in another part of the country. I rented out my flat but the tenants have moved out because they have suffered noise disturbance from neighbours. Can I take any legal action against these neighbours even though I don't live in the property?

A You certainly can. Any owner or occupier is entitled to take appropriate steps to put an end to any nuisance which affects their premises. In your case, a court order to control the noise is likely to be effective, or you can involve the local environmental officer if you prefer.

———

Q The other night we were driven mad by a car alarm. All the neighbours were disturbed but the car's owner could not be found. Can we do anything, legally, to stop this kind of noise?

A News of a brand new law will be music to your ears! Your local authority is empowered to operate a procedure to silence street noise and may set up a night-time 'noise line', which you can contact. For all long-suffering car alarm 'listeners', we really hope it works!

———

Q The son of one of my neighbours is always blocking the run-in to my garage. He was abusive when I asked him to move his car and the police refused to intervene, telling me that I have no legal right of entry to my own property. Can this be true?

A The police, as a matter of practicality, will not usually take action if your access *to* your property is blocked – only if you are prevented access *from* your house to the highway. In theory, any car on the highway can be moved for obstruction if the police deem it appropriate but, as a matter of policy, they consider taking steps only when rights to or upon the highway are interfered with, and not when entry to private property is hampered. Would it be possible for you to block your neighbour's garage to make them realize how uncooperative they are being? (See also pp. 24, 54.)

Q We like to sit in the garden in the summertime but our neighbour has recently acquired a huge dog which has twice jumped the boundary fence. The dog is not fierce but my wife is terrified of all dogs and she won't even let the children play out there. The neighbour claims that he is entitled to let the dog roam at will and therefore refuses to tie up his pet. Is he right?

A No. Cats are allowed to roam, not dogs. Your neighbour is guilty of trespass if his dog enters your garden and if he will not control the dog voluntarily, you may be forced to threaten legal action. You and your family are entitled to enjoy your garden as you please without unwanted intrusion. (See also pp. 25–30, 189, 207–8.)

Q Neighbours, whose garden backs onto ours, have planted hedges which – when fully grown – will obstruct our view of the lovely fields beyond their bungalow. Can we prevent the blocking of this vista which was one reason we bought our property?

A Unfortunately, there is no such thing as a legal right to a view. A friendly approach would seem the only way to tackle this potential problem. See whether you can persuade your neighbours to keep their hedges at a low level. (See also pp. 25, 34, 55.)

———

Q Two years ago, my husband agreed verbally with our neighbour to pay half the cost of a new fence between our houses. I knew nothing of this at the time and my husband and I are now separated, although the house is still in our joint names. My neighbour is now demanding the money from me. I can't afford to pay and cannot contact my husband. Am I liable?

A It is so important for married couples to discuss finances. We're sorry but you might well have to pay if it can be shown that, when your husband made the agreement, he made it on behalf of both of you by reason of the joint ownership of your house and the fact that this fence was of benefit to your jointly owned land. You can try to get out of paying but in the end it may be best to negotiate an instalment payment if you can. Incidentally, since the house is jointly owned, you really should try to track down your husband. He might have made other verbal agreements!

———

Q Can we stop our neighbour's son from putting cars in front of our house? He runs a car sales business from home and takes up the whole road with vehicles frequently blocking our garage entrance.

A Whilst anyone can lawfully park on a public highway, including outside your property, the police will only intervene if your car is blocked into its garage as this becomes an unlawful obstruction. However, to run a business from a private house requires planning consent and it might be worth mentioning to your neighbour's son the possible interest of the planning department unless he is more considerate of you in his business activities. (See also pp. 22, 32, 54.)

Q My wife dreams of an extension to our house but our neighbours are concerned that our proposals will block light from their back rooms. We don't think that their fears are justified but, equally, we don't want the expense of building now, only to face legal action later.

A With common sense and some good neighbourliness, there need be no problems. Go through the plans with your neighbours to reassure them and listen to their views. Since you must obtain planning permission before you build, this will give you protection against any later complaint. (See also pp. 24, 34, 55.)

Q We enjoy summer barbecues. Last year our next-door neighbour actually turned his hosepipe on the barbecue, hitting my wife with the full force of the water. To whom can we complain if he repeats this conduct this year, as he has threatened?

A What extraordinary behaviour! Yes – complain to the police for what amounts to an assault. If that doesn't do the trick, you could consider seeking legal advice to obtain a court order for what could amount to a trespass. (See also pp. 23, 27, 30.)

Q Our house has to be underpinned but our surveyor needs to carry out investigation from our neighbour's garden. Despite polite requests, we have been met by an adamant refusal to allow our surveyor to do the work. We are desperate as this work is vital. Is there anything we can do?

A Since the passing of legislation called the Access to Neighbouring Land Act 1991, it has been possible to get a court order to provide for necessary access to neighbouring land for situations just like yours. Make your application to your local county court without delay!

Q Our next-door neighbour has put up a fence between our garden and his. It's a very smart fence but the problem is that half our flower-bed has now disappeared into our neighbour's garden – about a one-foot strip of land. Although it is not very noticeable, we resent losing our property but our neighbour refuses to move the fence. How do we get our flower-bed back?

A If only people would discuss things with their neighbours, many lawyers would be out of work! First, see if you can find the original boundary fence line and, if so, point out to your neighbour that you can show his trespass. Failing that, long years of usage of land can sometimes be accepted as proof of boundaries. Be warned though, that if there is real doubt as to where the boundary lies, it can sometimes be more expensive to enter legal disputes than the lost land, itself, is worth. You might gain a foot and spend a fortune! (See also pp. 23, 30.)

Q Our neighbours pile junk in their front garden. The paint on their house is peeling, one window is boarded up and now the junction between our gutters is broken on their side so that water pours into the front wall of our house. What can we do about this eyesore?

A Well, the law can help a little but only to the extent that your neighbour is liable to fix the broken gutter to stop the water overflow to your property. If he refuses to do this, you will have to bear the cost yourselves and try to negotiate or sue for a contribution. As to the dumping ground complaint, you can do nothing about your neighbours' lifestyle as long as no physical damage is caused to your property or your family by any activity on their part. (See also pp. 30, 35.)

─────

Q The elderly gentleman living next door has just bought a Jack Russell terrier. I have a small baby and would like to leave him in the pram in the garden but I've heard that Jack Russells are known to attack babies and the dog can certainly get through our fence. Is there anything I can do to avert any danger in this situation?

A Talk to your neighbour, tell him your fears and see whether he intends to keep his dog under strict control. If he won't reassure you, you might consider a court order to stop any trespass by his dog into your garden. You might, too, build a more secure fence to protect your young baby from the dog and other dangers. (See also pp. 25, 58, 189, 207–8.)

─────

Q Water is coming into our house from our neighbour's leaking gutter. He refuses to fix it. Can we force him?

A You can certainly get a court order to have him fix the gutter and pay for any damage to your premises. However, do try to talk him round before going to court. After all, you do have to go on living next door to him. (See also pp. 30, 35.)

———

Q We moved into our new bungalow and discovered to our horror that we could hear every word spoken in the bungalow next door, which is linked to ours at bedroom level. The council's building inspectors confirmed that the builder had contravened building regulations and forced him to make amends. There are no problems now with noise but the builder has refused to compensate us for any stress and disturbance and we have lost some space in a bedroom and the bathroom because of the soundproofing. Do you think we are eligible for some compensation?

A Well, at least he's brought you and your neighbours into closer contact! Seriously, though, we think you are owed compensation. The builder's contract with you contains an implied guarantee that the building regulations have been complied with and you should be compensated for anything you suffer by his breach of that clause. Your best bet is to bring a small claims action in your local county or sheriff's court. You don't need a solicitor for this but your local citizens' advice bureau can advise and help.

———

Q We have fallen out with our next-door neighbours, who took exception to my husband cutting back their overhanging cherry trees even though the trees nearly reached our lounge window. Now we want to widen our drive but about three years ago the same neighbour planted some fir trees on our side of the drive which are in the way of the area to be widened. What advice do you have?

A Are you ready for the unpopular neighbour of the year award? Right – then get to work and pull up those trees which are trespassing on your land and have no right to be there. Nor indeed was your husband doing more than properly exercising his entitlement to cut back the cherry trees which, by overhanging your garden, became a legal 'nuisance'. (See also pp. 26, 33, 34.)

———

Q My son's neighbour is claiming the costs of damage to her back door which, she says, was caused by my son's labrador. The neighbour has a bitch which was in season when a number of dogs entered her garden through a hole in the back wall, although the neighbour insists that only my son's dog was seen. Must my son pay for this damage? His neighbour is threatening court action.

A If your son's dog was indeed responsible for the damage to the door, then he could well be held liable for the costs of repair if his dog was unrestrained and he was aware it was likely to enter the neighbour's garden when the next-door bitch was in season and cause the sort of damage complained of. However, the neighbour has first to prove that the labrador was the responsible 'party' and that it was not one of the other dogs whose owner she is unable to identify. (See also pp. 25–30, 58, 189, 207–8.)

———

Q Our next-door neighbours moved house and in their place a single young man moved in. Every time he goes out, he reverses his car over part of our front lawn, which is now looking decidedly the worse for wear. We have placed a plastic bollard near the spot and dropped a polite note through his letterbox asking him to drive more carefully, but so far nothing has changed. What legal steps, if any, can we take to let him know we mean business?

A Your thoroughly inconsiderate neighbour commits a trespass each time his car comes into contact with any part of your property. You are entitled to obtain a court order against him to prevent the trespass from continuing and you can claim damages for the 'wear and tear' to your lawn. A firm letter from you or, better still, a solicitor on your behalf, ought to make him realize what is in store unless he mends his ways. (See also pp. 25–29, 33–34.)

Q Our neighbour has cut down a large tree in his garden and allowed it to fall on our fence, damaging it and two shrubs. He has refused to pay for the damage to put it right. We would like to recover compensation but as our claim is only £50.00, we want to know the most economical way to go about this.

A Well, you've taken the first economical step by writing to us! The next best thing is to take proceedings in the 'small claims court' by going along to your local county court. The procedure is quite straightforward and, bearing in mind how much compensation you seek, the costs to you of issuing and pursuing the claim should be very modest indeed. (See also pp. 27, 28, 35.)

Q My neighbours have been away for several weeks and I thought they had returned early when I heard movements in the house. However, a few days ago, I realized that the house had been taken over by squatters. The police say they cannot act. Is there anything I can do to get these people out before my neighbours return and, if not, what remedy will my neighbours have? They will be horrified.

A You are clearly a good neighbour but unfortunately, that will not give you any rights to take action against these squatters. When your neighbours return and have recovered from their initial shock, they will be able to seek immediate relief from the courts by taking out proceedings to regain their property. It is not necessary for you or them to find out the precise identity of these squatters. Once a court order is obtained, the squatters can then be evicted, by bailiffs if necessary.

———

Q My neighbour has a Russian vine which grows very quickly and which he never bothers to cut back. Over the past few months, it has grown through his fence and is now taking over my garden too. Three times I have had to cut it back on my side of the fence. Can I force my neighbour to do this for me? Or, better still, can I make him take down the vine altogether?

A Both the vine and the dispute between you and your neighbour seem to be growing quickly. The growth into your garden is an encroachment which you are perfectly entitled to deal with as you have already done. Unfortunately, you cannot force your neighbour to be cooperative nor can you force him to remove the vine altogether. However, if you are seriously bothered by this state of affairs, you can work out the costs to you, in time and effort, of this pruning operation and charge it to him, suing if necessary through the local county court. He ought to get the message by then – but don't ever ask to borrow his lawn mower! (See also p. 35.)

———

Q My mother lives in a semi-detached house in a residential road. Next door the property is tenanted by a family whose son has recently been operating a disco in the downstairs room adjacent to my mother's lounge. The noise going on to the small hours every night is making my mother's life a misery – not only is it the loud music but the coming and going of cars and people. Her polite requests that the activity be limited has been met with abuse. Can she take any action short of starting court proceedings?

A She can and should report the matter without delay to the Housing or Planning Department of her local authority. Her neighbours are almost certainly in breach of the planning regulations governing the use of residential property and it is a safe bet that they have started the disco without the necessary planning permission to carry on such an activity. If they had applied for this, your mother would most certainly have known. The local authority have extensive powers to stop this activity and she should find them helpful and sympathetic. Only in the last resort should court proceedings be necessary to get an order against her inconsiderate neighbours. (See also p. 25.)

———

Q For some years now I have picked the apples from the overhanging branches of the next-door tree and made pies which my family enjoy. This summer, however, new neighbours moved in with whom we became quite friendly until the day when we had a heated exchange about my picking the apples, which they object to. Surely it can't be reasonable for them to make such a fuss as, after all, the apples do overhang our garden and my husband says I must be entitled to pick them.

A Apples seem to have been troublemakers since the world was created! No comment as to whether your neighbours are reasonable but, sorry, your husband is wrong. The apples on the tree remain your neighbours' property. You are entitled only to cut back the overhanging branches if you are so minded. Might we suggest that you restore good relations by offering to make one of your delicious pies for your neighbours in exchange for the apples. (See also pp. 31, 35.)

———

Q One of our local cats enjoys visiting his neighbours. One of the neighbours hates cats and chases him from her garden. That's her prerogative but she also throws stones at him when he's in my garden. I have objected without success. What can I do?

A The poor cat must be running out of lives! Before that happens, there is something you can do. Your protests at the cat's ill-treatment might get you nowhere but when someone throws anything, stones included, onto your property, that is actionable trespass which can and will be prevented by a county court or sheriff's injunction. And do tell the cat to steer clear of your neighbour's garden! (See also pp. 25–30, 34.)

———

Q I live in a row of terraced cottages which were built with access to the backs of the cottages at each end of the row.

The lady at one end has put up a high fence between her cottage and next door's which has blocked off not only her backyard but also everyone's access from her end of the row, making it inconvenient to get to the dustbins. She claims that she is entitled to keep this fence up.

A Well, she can keep the fence but she cannot block her neighbours' right to use the access. Either she provides a way through for everyone or the fence must come down. If she refuses to cooperate, then we suggest that you contact the planning department at your local authority to help you sort this out. (See also pp. 24, 25, 55.)

Q My next-door neighbour has taken up beekeeping. She has two hives at the bottom of her garden and all summer long the bees have swarmed over the fence and collected in our garden. My small daughters are terrified and now refuse to play outside. No one has been stung – yet – but we don't feel happy in our own garden with the bees about. Our neighbour has refused to discuss the problem. She says it's none of our business.

A It certainly is your business and your neighbour cannot tell you to buzz off! She might refuse to talk to *you* but if you report the matter to the pest control department at your local authority, she will have to talk to *them* and act upon any order they may make in relation to her hives. The beekeeping may also amount to a legal nuisance which can be dealt with by an application for an injunction at your local county court. (See also pp. 25–30, 33.)

Q While our next-door neighbours were on holiday, water leaked from one of their pipes into a room of our house, saturating our wall and carpet and soaking and ruining my husband's word processor and printer. After their return, the leak was repaired but their insurers refuse to pay for the damaged equipment, stating that the redecoration and new carpet is all they are liable for? Can we insist on payment?

A You have no direct rights against your neighbours' insurers but you are entitled to have all your claims met by your neighbours themselves. They seem to be properly insured for your claim and we would expect the insurers to pay you the value of the damaged equipment. But even if they are not, your neighbours are still liable to compensate you. (See also pp. 27, 28, 30.)

————

Q My next-door neighbour's garden is absolutely overgrown with weeds, including some poisonous growth which encroaches through our fence. Is there any way I can make him cut it back and tidy up his land?

A No, you cannot force your neighbour to take care of his garden. All you can do is cut back the weeds which spread onto your property. Why not ask him whether he'd like to borrow your shears? (See also pp. 32, 33.)

CHAPTER THREE

HOME, SWEET HOME

The adjective that derives from home is not 'homicidal', though that's often the way we feel in and about our abode. How pleasant it would be to close our front door and forget about the cares of the world. Unfortunately, an Englishman's home is not always his castle. Rapacious landlords, unruly tenants, cowboy builders, unscrupulous estate agents and door-to-door salesmen are all out to destroy our peace and privacy.

Who has and hasn't the right to enter our homes? What rights do we have as tenants? Are we responsible for the safety of invited visitors and workmen? In the following chapter we will give you advice on how to put the 'sweet' in 'home, sweet home!'

———

Q Do you have to have a solicitor when buying or selling a house? I was wondering whether I might do my own conveyancing. What do you think?

A You can do your own conveyancing but it would be very time-consuming. It could also carry certain risks, particularly regarding proof of title. It's probably better to use a lawyer for your own peace of mind. Even if you did do your own conveyancing, a building society would nominate its own lawyer to do its legal work. The cost of this would not be much different than if the solicitor carried out the conveyancing as well.

Q Our house was advertised for sale by local estate agents but then we changed our minds about wanting to sell and withdrew our instructions. Some weeks later, we have been approached by a couple who saw the advertisement and they have made us a good offer. If we do go ahead, would we have to pay the agents who, after all, are no longer acting for us and did very little to earn their commission?

A You are liable to pay the agents their commission since it was their advertising which, in fact, attracted your purchasers. We should add that estate agents always seem to have an uncanny knack of finding out about purchasers even when they have ceased acting for you. Why not come clean and see if you can negotiate with the agents on what will be an unexpected windfall for them if the sale goes through? (See also pp. 38, 40.)

Q We bought a newly built house. Part of the incentive to go ahead with the deal was the supply of carpets throughout. Over the last three years, lines have appeared on the carpets and now all the rooms are affected. The house building company agrees that there is a serious fault but says it is the responsibility of the carpet manufacturer, who has gone out of business. Can we do anything?

A If carpets were supplied as part of the whole deal when the house was bought, responsibility lies with the carpet suppliers, not the manufacturers. You should argue your rights under the Sale of Goods Act 1978 that the house builders supplied goods which were defective and replacement or compensation is due to you. (See also, pp. 121–24, 130–37.)

Q We bought our dream flat two months ago. We are just moving in and, to our horror, some of our furniture doesn't fit. The estate agent gave us a ground plan of the flat with measurements filled in and I'm afraid we didn't bother to measure up ourselves. Now we find our settee and dining table are too large for the rooms. My husband rang the estate agent and he just said the measurements were approximate, meant only as a guideline. Do we have any case against him? Our furniture is quite expensive as well as being what we like.

A Well, this is a word of warning to everyone not to take anything on trust when it comes to buying a property and to double-check everything yourself. That advice is a little late for you, unfortunately. Estate agents normally have exclusion clauses on their particulars which prevent would-be purchasers placing reliance upon the contents.

You have described a ground plan, however, which you may have been entitled to rely upon but it will be hard indeed for you to claim against the agent when you had every opportunity to check the measurements. Besides, from what you've said, it seems that you already had the furniture before you bought the flat: you did not buy the furniture relying on the measurements. You certainly do not seem to have any claim against the agent in respect of your purchase of the flat. (See also pp. 37, 40.)

————

Q We have just bought our house and are wondering what, legally, we can expect to find as fixtures and fittings when we move in.

A This is something which ought to form part of your contract with your seller. Legally, he must leave behind anything that cannot be removed without causing serious damage to the building or land to which it is attached. Apart from that, he can take out everything that he has not already agreed should remain and which has not been included in the sale price. If nothing is said about fixtures and fittings in the contract or sale negotiations, then you may find yourself in the same position as a friend of ours who arrived at night at her newly bought flat to find the vendor had taken everything down to the last light bulb. Not exactly the brightest of homecomings! However, the vendor was in breach only of the law of generosity, not in breach of contract.

————

Q We have just moved out of a flat which we rented for a year. We are entitled to be reimbursed £600 which we gave to the agent as a deposit, but the agency has since been sold and neither the original agent nor the new agent will return the money, each saying the other is responsible. Who is right?

A Since the money was paid to the first agent, it is he who should return it. If he, in turn, has a claim against the new agent, that is nothing to do with what he owes you. We hope you have a receipt for the deposit! (See also pp. 42, 43, 56, 100.)

———

Q We have recently bought a house and upon moving in we told the estate agents to take down their sign. They did so last week but as it had been nailed to weather-boarding at the front of the house, several slats appear to be quite seriously damaged where the sign was ripped off. Do we have any recourse and, if so, against whom?

A Your question raises a number of possible answers: first, if you are quite sure that the damage was caused by the removal of the sign, you could look to the estate agent for compensation. If, on the other hand, the *erection* of the sign was the cause of damage you would have a possible claim against both the agents and the former house owners, but only if the sign was put up after exchange of contracts. Any damage occurring before this crucial time would leave you with no remedy, since you are deemed to buy the house as you find it. (See also pp. 37, 39.)

———

Q I left my wife recently and moved into a flat which I rented on a year's lease. We are now reconciled and I want to go back to the family home but I am worried about the cost if I give up the flat now.

A Read your lease carefully. It may provide a notice period which allows you to bring the letting to an end before the year is up. If there is no such term, you will be liable for the rent on the unexpired period less any money received by the landlord if he chooses or is able to find another tenant for the remainder of your lease. (See also pp. 42, 43, 56, 100.)

Q Last year I was offered the chance to buy my flat for a good price as a sitting tenant. I have taken six months to make up my mind to buy and in that time the landlord has upped the price by £7,000. I am prepared to pay this but on condition he renovates my garage, which is in a sorry state. He refuses to do this. How do I stand, legally, on this matter?

A As a sitting tenant you cannot insist on the right to purchase the flat. It is up to your landlord whether he wants to sell to you and at what price. You are not, therefore, in a position to set conditions on the purchase – you can only negotiate and hope to find agreement. If it is still a good price, you ought to make up your mind before another six months go by and the price goes up yet again. (See also pp. 45, 51, 56, 100.)

Q My husband and I applied for and received an improvement grant from our local authority. The grant covered most of the cost of damp-proofing and wood treatment for our home. The problem is that the builders who carried out the work did not, in our opinion, do a good job and further work (and money) may be needed. The local authority officer nevertheless authorized payment to the builders, who have since gone into liquidation. Do we have any claim against the local authority as, by approving the payments, they appear to have also approved the work?

A There is no easy answer to this. The courts have recently decided that generally there is no liability on a local authority in respect of improvement grants since there is no duty of care to the person who receives the grant. Such a stance is justified because of the lack of control, in real terms, that the local authority have over your builders, who were at all times a party to a contract with you and your husband.

———

Q My husband has the opportunity to work abroad for a year. We are considering renting out our flat while we are away but I am concerned that we would have difficulty in getting the flat back from tenants when we return to England.

A If the flat has been your residence prior to the letting, then you would be entitled to possession of the property upon your return. We strongly advise, however, that you seek expert help in drawing up any tenancy agreement so as to ensure that you don't come home to problems. (See also pp. 39, 40, 45, 56.)

———

Q We bought a property and, since moving in, we have had nothing but problems: the ceilings in the bedrooms have come down; there is rising damp and the house smells musty. Our health is suffering and our lives are a misery owing to the condition of the house. We purchased the house with a mortgage from the building society who had a survey carried out but we were told nothing of the faults which must have been obvious. We are not eligible for a local authority grant and have no money to rectify the problems. Have we any remedy against the surveyor?

A You certainly would have a remedy against the surveyor, but only if you can show that he was negligent and failed to account for obvious faults when he carried out the survey.

We strongly urge you to seek advice from a solicitor but be warned – even if you succeed, your recovery may not cover the cost of the repairs and you could still be out of pocket.

Q I have almost completed the sale of my flat. How long will the solicitor hold the money?

A Provided everything is in order, the Law Society says the money should reach you on completion. If it does not, you are due for interest on the money held. If you have any cause for complaint, write to the Solicitors' Complaints Bureau, Portland House, Stag Place, London SW1E 5BL.

Q For the past three years, I have been a tenant occupying the ground floor flat of a house. I have just found out that the landlord has defaulted on his mortgage to the building society who are seeking possession through the court of the whole property. The mortgage, it seems, was granted last year and my landlord 'forgot' to tell them of my tenancy. I seem to be facing eviction and am desperate. What can I do?

A You should make your position known quickly! Inform the building society of your tenancy and how long you have been there. Find out from them the date of the court action and go along there on the day as an 'intervening party', i.e. one affected by an order likely to be made. On the facts here, you look to have full protection as the mortgage was given after your tenancy and the building society cannot now gain vacant possession of the property. The position would be very different if your tenancy had started after the mortgage had been granted. In your case, it would seem that you cannot be evicted and if the property is sold, you remain the tenant with a new, and hopefully, more scrupulous landlord. (See also pp. 39, 40, 51, 100.)

———

Q For the last twenty years, I have shared a flat with my brother who died six months ago. He had lived in the flat for ten years prior to my moving in. Although the tenancy was in his name, we split rent and all other expenses down the middle. Two months after his death, I had a letter from the owners of the property, saying they wanted vacant possession within two months. The company is registered in the Dutch West Indies. I consulted a solicitor and he told me that if I wanted to fight the case, Counsel's opinion would have to be sought. I gave him £500 to cover costs.

The case is waiting to come to court and I haven't yet had an opinion as to the likely outcome. I'm scared stiff as if I get evicted, I've nowhere to go. The council has a waiting list for accommodation and can only offer me bed and breakfast. I hate the thought of this. I'd have to put my furniture in store and share a kitchen.

The flat I've lived in for so long is worth about £100,000 now as it's in a gentrified area. I couldn't begin to afford it and it seems unfair that we've paid a fair rent for thirty years and lived in the neighbourhood all our lives and now I'm being pushed out by a wealthy property company.

A We could not agree more. After all those years, to face this uncertainty is unacceptable. However, it is possible that the opinion, when it comes, may be of comfort to you. From what you've told us you might come within the provisions of the Housing Act 1988, which allows a member of the family of the tenant to inherit the tenancy in certain circumstances. As a brother you qualify as a member of the family and as you lived in the flat for over the two-year qualifying period, it looks like you're all right there too.

The cloud on the horizon concerns the type of tenancy your brother had. Under the Act of 1988 you can inherit only a statutory tenancy that is, a tenancy that came into existence after an original tenancy, for a term of years, had ended. If the tenant remained in place and continued to pay rent and if that was the position with your late brother then you could have protection from eviction.

If, however, your brother did not have a statutory tenancy then you may find yourself vulnerable to a court order for possession of your home and regrettably you will have to face the alternatives available: either rehousing by the council, however unpalatable; or consider some sort of flat share and lodgings, which may be preferable.

We sympathize with you and wish you well whatever the outcome. (See also pp. 51, 53, 56, 100.)

———

Q We have rented a flat but the landlord insisted that we sign a document describing the letter as a 'licence'. There is no fixed term for our letting and the flat is self-contained, but we are concerned that by signing this document, the landlord can evict us at any time without good reason.

A A tenancy by any other name is still a tenancy! If you have exclusive possession of the flat and there is no provision for the landlord to have unrestricted access to the premises, then you almost certainly have the full protection of tenants under the Rent Acts and calling your letting a 'licence' is but a transparent attempt by the landlord to get around your rights! If you have any doubts about your tenure, take your letting agreement to your local citizens' advice bureau or law centre. They will settle the matter for you. (See also pp. 41, 42, 56, 100.)

Q We bought an eighteenth-century cottage this year and had the walls injected against damp and then plastered. Unfortunately, the damp has seeped through and the surveyor says this is because the builder used the wrong plaster. The builder, for his part, says we didn't let the plaster dry out properly and absolutely refuses to do the repair work without further payment. Can we rely on the surveyor's report and force him to do the work at no more cost to us, or will we have to employ another builder?

A You can certainly rely on the surveyor's report, but if the builder still refuses to provide his services without charge, you can't force him to carry out any extra work. What you can do is to get another builder and then use the surveyor and his report as the basis of a claim against the first builder to recover the cost of redoing the work – if it is proved and accepted that it was defective work in the first place, as your surveyor believes.

Q Do I have any remedy against a builder who now refuses to carry out work at the price agreed on his estimate? He claims that he costed the work below its value and insists that I agree to an increase before he will undertake the job.

A The builder is in breach of contract by insisting on an increase and, whilst you cannot force him to carry out the job at the original price agreed, you are entitled to employ another builder to do the work to the same standard. However, if you now have to pay more for the work you can look to the original builder to compensate you for the difference. (See also p. 121.)

———

Q We had builders in to erect an extension to the back of our house but halfway through the work they simply abandoned us. We made enquiries and discovered that the company had gone into liquidation. We have now had estimates of twice the price to finish the job. Where do we stand?

A Regrettably, you stand right in the middle of an expensive mess. Unfortunately for you, if the company is no longer operating then there is little point in pursuing them. Find out if a receiver has been appointed and, if so, whether there is any chance that he is managing any works for the company. In that case, you can entreat him to get your extension completed. If not, then you will just have to pay up or live with a half-finished extension. You may think it worthwhile to lodge a claim with the liquidator in the hope of recovering some of the increased cost of the work.

———

Q Is there anything I can do to prevent any future owners of my house from tearing down ivy which houses a wren's nest or from cutting down a delightful cherry blossom tree? I am thinking of moving but I would like to feel that these items are protected if I sell up.

A You might be able to persuade a buyer of your home to enter an agreement, as a special condition of sale, not to interfere with either the ivy or the tree. However, such an agreement could affect the sale price of your property or even put off a purchaser altogether and, in any case, it would not bind any subsequent purchaser of the house. Sometimes the local authority will put preservation orders on certain trees to prevent them being cut down, but we doubt that they would put such an order on a cherry blossom tree. Your only hope is that future residents of your house enjoy it as much as you do and will not want to change it.

———

Q A huge lime tree is growing on the pavement outside my house and I am sure it is causing structural damage to the house as well as depriving us of daylight. The local council refuses to fell. What can I do about it?

A If the tree is simply depriving you of daylight, you have no remedy. If, however, you have good reason to believe that your property is being adversely affected then you should first seek expert advice from a surveyor. If your suspicions turn out to be accurate and the tree is causing or likely to cause damage, you may be able to take court action against the council, requiring them to fell it. If damage has already been caused, the council may well be liable for the cost of remedial work but you will need detailed legal advice to pursue that one. (See also pp. 52, 204.)

———

Q My boyfriend and I are in the process of buying a house but one thing bothers me. If my boyfriend dies, who will get his share of the house? My boyfriend says I will but I think it will be his next of kin, i.e. his mother. And there's no way I would want to share my house with her! I certainly hope nothing happens to either of us for a long time yet, but can you put my mind at rest?

A It is very sensible that you sort this out now. When you buy your house, make sure that it is purchased as a joint tenancy with a right of survivorship. This ensures that the whole property passes to whichever of you survives the other. That way his mother won't even get a foot in the door! We do stress that you make sure you tell your solicitor exactly what you want at the time of the purchase since this intention as to title has to be clearly stated on the transfer document. (See also pp. 89, 92, 96, 98.)

———

Q My boyfriend and I bought a house in joint names eight years ago. It was a bargain as it was in a terrible state and we've since done it up. The neighbourhood has also gone up in the world so it's now worth a lot more. The problem is I've fallen for someone else, he wants to marry me and I like the idea suddenly. I want us to sell the house and go halves on the money but my boyfriend flatly refuses. He says he wants to stay in the house and will give me half of what we originally paid for it. This is obviously ridiculous. Can he do this?

A No, he cannot! You are entitled to half its market value and, in your case, you can make an application to the court for a declaration as to your half share *and* an order for the sale of the house. (See also pp. 7, 9, 11, 13.)

———

Q My boyfriend wants me to give up my council flat and move into his house with a view to marriage. I am uncertain as to whether I want to marry him but I am tempted to move in as he is willing to put his house into our joint names 'as a sign of good faith'. If I do move in but then do not marry him will I be entitled to claim a share in the house if we separate in the future?

A Not necessarily, is the short answer. It all depends upon the intention behind the transfer of the property. If it is your boyfriend's intention to make a gift to you of a share in his property, you would probably be able to establish a claim. If, however, the transfer was with a view only to marriage, then you might end up with nothing. It is essential, then, that the exact basis of your moving in and any transfer made is clearly spelled out – preferably with the advice and assist-ance of a solicitor *and* before you give up the security of your council home. (See also pp. 7, 9, 12, 13.)

Q Six years ago, I left my rented flat to move in with my boyfriend. He is buying his house on a mortgage. It is in his name and he pays it but we go halves on all the outgoings and I reckon I buy most of our food and drink. This didn't matter except we've been quarrelling a lot and are now splitting up. The trouble is that I've not enough to pay a deposit on a place of my own and the cost of rented accommodation has soared beyond my means. My ex-lover says it's not his problem and will give me nothing although we bought some of the furniture jointly. What is my legal position?

A Apart from the furniture which you bought together and therefore own jointly, we're sorry to tell you that you have secured no property rights for yourself by paying bills or household expenses as you are not married. The court has no power to make transfer of property orders in the case of cohabitation and you can, therefore, expect nothing unless you have legal title to it. (See also pp. 7, 9, 11, 13.)

––––––

Q My son lives at home and drives me mad. He does not pay for his keep. He stays up all night, leaving heaters and lights on. He makes a mess of the house and he is unpleasant and uses foul language to both my husband and myself. He says he doesn't care for any of us and his moodiness and unpleasantness is causing distress to both my husband and myself. He is now twenty-eight. Is there any way we can get him to leave?

A Your son has only a licence to occupy your house and whichever of you or your husband owns the house can simply withdraw this licence. However, we strongly urge you to do this in writing and by means of a solicitor's letter, which will be sufficient to bring your son's occupancy to an end and hopefully give you and your husband the peace and tranquillity that you clearly desire. However, from what you say, we wonder whether you should be persuading your son to see a doctor? If he won't, you will have to prepare yourselves for possible ugly scenes if you take steps to evict him. (See also pp. 41, 44, 45, 100.)

––––––

Q I have a South American woman working for me as a cleaner once a week. She is very pleasant and I'm satisfied with her work but I have this nagging suspicion that she is an illegal immigrant. She came to me on a friend's recommendation; she got her in reply to her advertisement in the local paper. My friend is not bothered but I feel dreadful about it. I'm against breaking the law and people living illegally here. I'll probably give her notice but I wonder, what would be the situation if she is an 'illegal'? Would I be an accessory after the fact?

A There is no such concept as an 'accessory after the fact' in English law. If you arrange or encourage a criminal offence (and illegal immigration is an offence) then you are a principal along with the offender.

However, casual employment of a cleaner who you may suspect is not going to involve you in any criminal offence and giving her notice and thus setting your mind at rest is probably your best option although you could, of course, report your suspicions to the Home Office.

Q We live in a council house and an elderly visitor tripped over on the path leading to our front door. The path was broken up by council workmen when they were working on pipes below the front garden and, despite our numerous complaints, they failed to reinstate the paving. As we occupy the house and the path leads to our premises, does our visitor have any claim against us, or can she sue the council for her injury?

A The council normally retains control over the structure and outsides of its properties. If, as is likely, they have an obligation to maintain and repair premises let by them, then your visitor would certainly have a claim against them for their failure to meet their obligation in respect of the path, especially as you had actually complained to them about it. (See also pp. 48, 204.)

Q Our cleaning lady slipped and fell on our rather highly polished floor last week. Fortunately, she was perfectly all right, especially after a large brandy! But it did set me wondering as to what the position is if a cleaner or window cleaner has an accident in your home. Would one be liable?

A If a visitor to your home has an accident (and a visitor includes any person who lawfully comes to your house), then there is a potential liability for any injury or loss suffered. However, you would only be liable if the injury is caused by some negligence on your part and your household insurance policy may well cover you for this type of situation. If you have such a policy – read it! And tell your cleaning lady not to polish your floors so efficiently! (See also p. 72.)

Q We live in a rented flat which is one of a number in a large converted house. For months now we have endured constant flooding from our toilet, which is unpleasant as well as creating mess and aggravation every time it occurs. The fault lies somewhere in the pipes which serve all the flats and it seems that attention needs to be given to the plumbing in the flat upstairs before our problem is cured. We know this because, despite telephone calls, personal visits and letters, our landlord, who is responsible for all repairs, has ignored us and we ended up paying for a plumber ourselves who was unable to cure the problem. We are at our wits' end and we wonder whether to resort to sending a solicitor's letter to the landlord to make him act. We don't know what else we can do!

A A landlord like yours would be just as likely to ignore a solicitor's letter as he has ignored your letters and calls. An order obtained by you in your local county or sheriff's court is more likely to achieve the desired response and you can seek assistance from either the court office or, better still, your local law centre or citizens' advice bureau.

Have you thought of having a word with the occupier upstairs? If he, too, is a tenant, he might join forces with you against the landlord. He might even clear up the faulty plumbing himself or pay for or towards the cost of your plumber to do the work – so you can at least know it's done. You can claim the cost from your landlord if he is obliged to carry out the repairs under the terms of your tenancy agreement. (See also pp. 40–45.)

_____

Q Is there anything I can do about the persistent parking outside my house? Often the same cars appear and sometimes my garage entrance is actually blocked, although for the most part the vehicles are positioned so as to make it as awkward as possible for me to get my own car in and out of the drive.

A Apart from heartfelt sympathy, we can offer precious little comfort. If you reside on a designated public highway you can do nothing to stop legitimate parking, however awkward it may be for you. However, if you find your drive actually blocked, this does constitute an actionable obstruction and your local police may well assist in finding the offender and may even prosecute. If you want to resort to it, you can bring a civil action for nuisance against persistent and known 'blockers'. A cautionary tale here: a fellow sufferer complained vociferously to the local council who 'helpfully' responded by painting yellow lines all down his road; both he and his neighbours wish he had suffered in silence! (See also pp. 23, 25.)

_____

Q My parents live close to a youth club and on several occasions damage has been caused to their and neighbours' cars by the people attending. They have contacted the police and numerous councillors to try to get the club closed, but to no avail. Please have you any suggestions as to what action they can take next?

A It looks as if the only course open to your parents and their neighbours is to try to pressurize the local authority to impose a change of user of the premises so that the club can no longer operate. If the premises are licensed, they may be able to raise sufficient objections to the renewal of this licence when it is next due. Regrettably, there seems no further remedy available as there is no liability on the part of the club for damage caused on the public highway – unless the persons responsible for the damage were acting on behalf of the club.

———

Q Remember the man who put a shark on his roof and the African woman who built a mud hut in her garden? Well, the man across the street has obviously been inspired by them. He's put a huge, model aeroplane on his roof. It's amusing for five minutes then it's an eyesore. We've complained to the council but we've not had much joy from them.

A The aeroplane may be an eyesore but only if it also offends local planning rules relating to roof lines will the local authority act. If the aeroplane is within lawful planning laws then all you can hope for is another hurricane which will blow the plane off course. We wonder whether, if everyone in the street put up something on their roofs, the local council might do something about it. (See also pp. 24, 25, 34.)

———

Q Eighteen months ago, my parents remortgaged their house and took out endowment insurance cover at the same time. My father was then suffering with a heart condition from which he died two months later. The insurers have refused to pay off the mortgage, claiming that the cover was only on my mother's life. My mother is struggling to meet the payments and she is sure the insurance covered my father's life as well. Do we have any redress?

A Normally, an endowment policy to pay off an outstanding mortgage operates in the event of the death of either party to a mortgage. It may be that, because your father's poor health was known to the insurers, they would only cover your mother's life. You should have a close look at the terms of the insurance and find out exactly what was agreed at the time. You may need the advice of a solicitor.

We cannot stress too often the need to read documents carefully, however boring they might be. The small print can hide big problems!

Q We rent our home and our landlord is hopeless. He has promised to send a plumber to mend a leaky radiator for weeks but despite reminders to him nothing has been done. Can we withhold rent until he fulfils his obligation to carry out this repair?

A Technically, you would be in breach of the terms of your lease if you refuse to pay rent however tempting this may be. The better course for you is either to have the work done yourself and then deduct the cost from your rent, after first warning the landlord of your intent to do this, or to threaten court action to force him to have the work done. (See also pp. 39, 40, 41, 42, 45.)

———

Q Some months ago my husband and I bought an old cottage in the country which had some outbuildings erected before we moved in. Now our neighbours are complaining that one of the walls of the outbuildings is responsible for cracking their sewer pipe and this had led to rats entering their garden. The outbuildings were not put up by us and we don't even use them. Can we be held responsible for what is happening?

A And you thought you escaped the rat race when you moved to the country! This could well be your responsibility if the damage to the pipe has occurred since you purchased the cottage. You will have to try to find out discreetly or otherwise if any similar complaint by your neighbours was being made before you bought the cottage. That would be one way of showing that the problem existed before you moved in. If it can be shown that damage was caused before your purchase of the cottage, the previous owner could well be responsible to your neighbours. In any event, whenever the damage occurred, you might be able to recover any loss from him – depending upon whether he gave accurate and full answers to enquiries made by your solicitors when you bought the property. You need expert advice here – from both a solicitor and a surveyor – and you should take a close look at your insurance position.

———

Q My boyfriend and I are planning to buy a house together. I want us to marry but he says we can get a better mortgage if we don't. Is he right?

A Name the day! Since August 1988, there is no advantage to be gained by a couple each retaining their single status to obtain the tax relief on a mortgage. So, no excuses for reluctant brides or bridegrooms – married or single, two can live as cheaply as two!

Q We have a guard dog so I'm not worried about break-ins. What worries me is what happens if the dog bites a visitor to the house.

A You have a duty to warn all visitors of the presence of the dog and the dog must be sufficiently controlled or under restraint to ensure the safety of everybody who comes to your premises lawfully. (See also pp. 27, 29, 189, 207–8.)

Q I've been trying to sell my flat for well over a year with no success. I read that someone organized a raffle to sell theirs and wonder what the problems might be if I decided to do the same?

A A major pitfall is that it is illegal! The case you read about was probably the man in Ireland who sold £5 raffle tickets and finally unloaded his property.

What is possible in Britain is to arrange a competition so that a game of chance becomes a game of skill. Competition entry forms are filled in and paid for like a ticket and if you sell enough you then have your flat as the prize, having achieved its price through competition entry sales.

The main things to watch for are:

(1) to ensure good organization of ticket sales;

(2) to organize a genuine competition of skill that does not fall foul of the law;

(3) most importantly, to have a 'get out' clause so that if you fail to achieve ticket sales to a sufficient value, you can call off the competition and keep your flat;

(4) take advice if in any doubt.

Best of luck to you!

CHAPTER FOUR

CHILDREN

'May all your problems be little ones!' is the traditional wedding toast. And, oh, how often they are!

Problems with children are not always their fault, of course. They can cause us heartache and grief if they're badly behaved but they can suffer at the hands of bullies, be held back at school or find themselves in the middle of marital disputes.

There are so many situations with children where you need to know your (and their) rights. Is their school insured against accidents on the premises? Does your child *have* to visit your ex-husband even if he doesn't want to? What rights, if any, do surrogate mothers have? What can we do to make sure our children are as happy and well treated as they ought to be?

———

Q I am a sperm donor. There is just one thing that worries me about this and that is, what happens if a law is brought in giving children born as a result the right to know the identity of their father? I have a family of my own and I have no desire to be involved in the future of the children born as a result of my donations. If I write a will specifying this, can I ensure that, if the worst happened and a child was given my details, he or she would not inherit?

A A sperm donor is not to be treated as the father of a child where the method of A.I.D. (Artificial Insemination by Donor) has been used. When such a child reaches eighteen, application for information as to ethnic origin, genetic health and background may be sought from a register where these details are kept, but the identity of the sperm donor is not and cannot be given.

Should the law change to allow for the child to know who his 'sperm father' is, then you can protect yourself by excluding any such child in your will and, assuming the child has had no financial dependence on you in your lifetime, he or she could not challenge such a will.

———

Q My sister can't have children. A year ago she unwisely agreed to a friend of hers having a baby for her. The friend was promised a lump sum when the baby was born and lived with them for the last three months of her pregnancy. Now what I always feared has happened; the baby has been born but my sister's friend won't give it up. She claims that, as no legal contract was ever signed and no money was exchanged, my sister has no rights over the child even though my brother-in-law is the father. What can my sister do?

A Unhappily, your sister can do nothing at all. She has no legal right to this child and your brother-in-law has only the right to apply for contact or residence, as would any father of a 'non-marital' child. (See also p. 69.)

Q We've longed for a child for many years without success. We've been turned down for adoption on the grounds of age. Now, an American friend has told me that she can buy a baby for us in South America. I know the word 'buy' seems awful but we would love and cherish a child, believe me. I want our friend to go ahead but my husband is worried about the legal implications. If we bring the child here, can we register him or her as our own? Would the baby be a British subject and entitled to a British passport eventually? Please advise us of any pitfalls which might arise.

A One immediate problem would be if the baby had been obtained from a notorious 'baby farm' and its natural mother sought its return. No British court would recognize any contract to 'buy' a child as legal or binding and we doubt you would have much chance to keep the child if the mother sought its return – nor would you get your money back.

However, if a legal and genuine adoption can be undertaken in the child's country of origin, then the practical arrangements are that the child receives authorized entry papers for admission to the UK which are probably for some six months' duration initially but can be renewed. You must work with the Official Solicitor or, in Scotland, a curator appointed by the court, who represents the child's interests and an independent social worker who will liaise with the Official Receiver (or curator) and the courts. Eventually, an adoption is arranged in this country after which, of course, the child acquires British citizenship and is entitled to be treated in all ways as your natural child. (See also p. 69.)

——

Q My husband and I are unable to have children of our own and we have been turned down for adoption because of our ages (we are in our late thirties) and because we follow different religions (this has never caused any friction between us, I think I may say we are very tolerant people). Recently, I got to know a young, unmarried mother of an adorable two-year-old daughter. She would like to go to London to make a fresh start and we would love to adopt the child. Is this possible to arrange? The girl is willing but are there any snags to a private adoption, like the mother claiming her back sometime in the future?

A You are not, unfortunately, able to arrange a private adoption and have it sanctioned by the court in these circumstances. All adoptions of children in the United Kingdom have to be approved through a recognized adoption agency. Your only hope might be to have the mother give you actual custody of her child; if the child lives with you as effective foster parents for at least five years, you might then be able to go through with an adoption. Of course, the risks of this are obviously that the mother could reclaim her child and you are by no means guaranteed an adoption at the end of the five years. (See also p. 69.)

——

Q I am a fourteen-year-old girl and I'm sick and tired of living with my parents. They are always rowing, so much so that I sometimes get scared. Then they make up and tell me not to be silly as that's just the way they are. I don't feel I belong at home at all.

My two girl cousins have a smashing mum and dad and I know they'd be happy to take me in. I spend masses of time there anyway. I'm sure my parents wouldn't object but how can I persuade them?

A You might well find they'll be bitterly hurt when you tell them you don't want to live at home any more.

You are, of course, too young to leave home of your own volition. You can't do that till you're sixteen.

Your aunt and uncle might not mind having you as a visitor but are you sure they would want you permanently?

There are so many things involved here. Would you still be able to go to the same school, for instance? What financial arrangements would have to be made? The legal situation is this: you are entitled to have your wishes heard by a court and you can, in your own right, seek legal aid for guidance and advice by a solicitor. Under the Children Act, the court must take account of your views as to where you wish to reside and, if it is both desirable and appropriate, it is indeed possible for you to obtain a 'divorce' from your parents.

However, there have already been cases where such a 'divorce' has not proved entirely successful and where the children concerned have learned that the grass on the other side of the fence was not so much greener after all.

Q My son, aged eight, was injured at a local firework display when a Catherine Wheel ricocheted off a tree and hit him. He was standing at the front of a crowd of children who had all been 'organized' into position by those responsible for the display. The organizers have refused to accept responsibility and state that the firework must have been defective.

Can I seek compensation for my son who has a nasty scar on his forehead and, if so, from whom?

A The organizers of such a display must be aware of their responsibilities to those invited or paying to watch. If onlookers are allowed to stand too close or the fireworks are ignited into a crowd, any injury resulting is the liability of those in charge if it is shown that the incident was caused by their insufficient care in setting up the display.

If the firework was indeed defective, as is claimed here, then the supplier could be liable although ultimate responsibility lies with the manufacturer, to whom an injured party could look for compensation.

In the first instance, you should write to the organizers setting out your complaints. If you get no joy from them, you should then get in touch with the fireworks' manufacturers, if you know who they are. If this all fizzles out like a damp squib, go to your local law centre or citizens' advice bureau. (See also pp. 66, 72, 78, 107.)

Q Since he was ten, our fifteen-year-old son has wanted to be a lawyer and his father and I are very keen to encourage him. Our problem is that he runs around with a gang at school who are always up to some mischief. They don't commit any serious crimes but one of the boys was caught stealing a packet of cigarettes and was cautioned by a police officer. If our son had been involved, how would this have affected him and his ambition?

A Police officers do prefer to caution youngsters in these circumstances but, on the whole, it's best not to risk any kind of record whether you want to be a barrister or a barman!

Children under the age of seventeen can only be cautioned if they admit guilt and if the parents consent. The child, accompanied by a parent, is brought before a senior police officer and given a warning that if he commits any more offences, he is likely to be taken to court. This usually has a deterring effect and we're sure your child will not wish to reach that point. A caution, however, is not a conviction and need not be disclosed as such.

———

Q My partner is being assessed for child maintenance of his children who live with his ex-wife. Can the Child Support Agency take account of my income in working out what he has to pay for them?

A When the assessment is made, the agency is entitled to make certain deductions from your partner's claimed outgoings according to a set formula which makes allowance for your contributions. None of your actual income can be applied directly for the maintenance payments. (See also pp. 16, 17.)

———

Q My ten-year-old was pushed over in his school playground on the last day of the summer term. He fractured his thumb, which meant that he was unable to go on a canoeing trip arranged by the local youth centre. He was bitterly disappointed and I've had to pay the cancellation fee for the trip. Can I claim it from the school?

A School authorities are generally not insured for simple accidental injury, although if the injury occurs by reason of negligence and incompetence on the part of the school then a claim might be feasible. Find out the insurance position of the school and also the circumstances of your son's accident to see if, indeed, you have grounds for compensation. (See also pp. 65, 72, 78, 107.)

———

Q My little daughter, aged six, was hit in the face by a stone during playtime at her school. Some children, it seems, were playing nearby and throwing sticks and stones but no teacher was there to supervise. She was lucky not to lose her eye but it looks like she may have a permanent scar on her face. I am very upset about this. Is there anything I can do?

A What an unfortunate occurrence! If there was no super-vision at all then you could show inadequate care being taken by the school. If, however, supervisors were about but just happened to miss a one-off throw, then it will not be quite so easy to show that there was lack of reasonable super-vision. After all, the school can't provide watchers for each child all of the time. Since you suggest that the stone-throwing had been going on for a while, it ought, if a careful watch was being kept, to have been stopped. In short, depending on the facts, you may well have a good case against the school authorities for claiming compensation on behalf of your daughter.

———

Q My brother has lived with his girlfriend for ten years and they have just had a little girl. Does he have to adopt his own daughter in order to establish he's her father, or does he have the same rights as any married father?

A Under the Children Act 1989, your brother can make a formal agreement with his girlfriend to share parental responsibility for their child. This will ensure that he has full rights as if he were married to the mother. Even if such an agreement is not reached, your brother has the right to be heard by any court considering the future care of the child, should the parents split up.

Q My second husband and I have been married for eight years. We have two lovely children and my ten-year-old daughter from my first marriage lives with us. We're all so happy together that I'd like Susie to take my husband's surname so we can all feel like one family. Is this possible?

A It is possible but only if Susie's father is agreeable or the court sanctions the change. There usually has to be an exceptional reason to permit a child to be known by another name. An almost complete assimilation into a new family structure, as appears to be your case, might well suffice but do talk to your first husband about it first. (See also pp. 4, 70, 213.)

Q After extensive testing, my husband and I have been told that we will not be able to have a child. The problem lies with me and I am depressed beyond words. Now a friend has agreed to enter into a surrogacy arrangement – she will (hopefully) become pregnant by my husband. Assuming all goes well, where do we stand as parents when the baby is born and handed over to us?

A You have to adopt the child formally before you will be its parents legally and you and your husband have to be acceptable to the adoption agencies and social services even though your husband is the 'natural' father. So you could find yourselves heartbroken at the end of the day if the authorities refuse to sanction the adoption. However, if the baby is with you soon after the birth and you are obviously loving, caring and able to provide a suitable home, it is likely (but not certain) that you will be able to go ahead with the adoption. (See also pp. 62, 63.)

———

Q My fiancé is divorced and his ex-wife has custody of their small daughter who recently started school. He has discovered that the child has been enrolled at the school in her mother's maiden name and, although he has complained, the school refuses to do anything about it. He is really upset and wants to know if he can achieve anything by going to court about this.

A Your fiancé's ex-wife is not entitled to change the surname of their child without good reason or his consent. Without delay, your fiancé can seek a court order against his ex-wife to ensure that his daughter is known both at school and generally by the name on her birth certificate. (See also pp. 4, 70, 213.)

———

Q Do I have the right to see my grandchildren? I have fallen out with my daughter-in-law and she is trying to stop me seeing the children, but I am prepared to go to court if necessary to maintain contact with them. Would the court help me?

A The court will only consider an application by you if there already exists a court order regarding the legal custody of your grandchildren (following a divorce, for example) or where one of the children's parents (or both) is deceased. Another, but remote, possibility would be for you to attempt to have the children made wards of court and then apply for contact but your chances of success are slight and you would be unlikely to get legal aid. Hard for you though it is, your best solution is to swallow hard and try to make it up with your daughter-in-law – for yours and the children's sakes. (See also pp. 71, 80.)

———

Q Five years ago, I had an affair with a man and had his child. I registered him in my name. Now the father has come back into my life and we want to be together. For financial reasons, I do not want to marry him but we are going to spend the rest of our lives together. We want Sam to have my lover's surname now. Can we change it on the birth certificate?

A Once a birth certificate is completed, it is virtually impossible to alter any details on it. Therefore, your surname will remain on Sam's certificate but you can change his name by deed poll if you so wish. This, of course, applies to anyone wishing to change their name for whatever reason. (See also pp. 4, 68, 69, 213.)

———

Q My girlfriend did not put my name on our son's birth certificate. He is now sixteen and has asked to come to live with me. It's what I want. He calls himself by my surname but I would like it to be official. Is it possible to change his birth certificate since that's what he wants too?

A Your son cannot change his birth certificate. All he can do is change his name officially by deed poll when he is eighteen and this is registered. One father we know provided a misspelt version of his son's name to the birth registry and had to beg and plead with them to correct it one week after the boy's birth. Hopefully a deed poll change will provide the solution though this could not be entered on the original birth certificate, which is sacrosanct. (See also pp. 4, 68, 213.)

———

Q My son and his wife have separated and she has subsequently suffered a nervous breakdown. The social workers in charge of the 'case' are talking about our grandchild being taken into care. My husband and I adore the child and would love to have her live with us. Would it be possible for us to put forward our case in court?

A Why wait till it reaches that stage? Why not contact the social worker in charge, explain how much you would like to take the child and state your case for having her live with you. To answer your question, though, magistrates can rule that grandparents may be parties to care proceedings. But even if you are not, the court has power to award you care and control if it is considered to be in the best interests of your grandchild and under the Children Act 1989 you can apply to be made parties to proceedings. (See also pp. 70, 80.)

———

Q On a lovely sunny day, we drove to the coast for a day out. We stopped for a meal at a large service area with playground equipment. Our small daughter went on the slide and fell off sideways because a support at the top was missing. She was shocked more than hurt but the manager was most unsympathetic and said it was our fault for not supervising her. There was a notice disclaiming responsibility but supposing she had been seriously injured?

A If your daughter had been hurt due to damaged or defective equipment in the play area, then all the disclaimer notices in the world would not protect those responsible for the playground. However, small children should be closely watched in playgrounds because accidents do happen and if supervision is not provided, children's safety is a parental responsibility. (See also pp. 65, 67.)

———

Q We are having an extension built and a small cement mixer is temporarily in our front garden. Our neighbour is concerned for the safety of her son who plays outside but surely she has the responsibility to keep him out of our property?

A Your neighbour has primary responsibility for her son's safety but if you have dangerous machinery on your premises which could attract a child, you could well find yourself liable for injury if you have not taken sufficient steps to keep out a small, inquisitive trespasser. (See also p. 53.)

———

Q We have been divorced three years and our seven-year-old son lives with me. He goes to the local, very good, state school and is happy there. Now my ex-husband says he wants Tom to go to his old school where boys in his family have gone for four generations. I don't want Tom to go away to school. Also, I believe in state education (one of the bones of contention between my husband and me). My ex-husband says he will fight me on this and says he will win because he has the right to decide and pay for his child's education. Is this right?

A Your husband has equal parental responsibility for Tom and, strictly speaking, he has *as much* not *more* – say than you about his son's education. An issue like this could end up the subject of court hearings and, while Tom's interest and happiness will be of paramount importance, you have to be on guard that a court might regard his interest as being the fifth generation at the old school. If, however, it means his being at boarding school, as you indicate, your ex might have a tougher fight on his hands, particularly if you have greater residence rights over Tom which means it was considered appropriate that he live with you – not at school. (See also p. 79.)

———

Q I have every reason to believe that my daughter has been put into a class which undermines her academic capabilities. She attends a multiracial school and many of her classmates have little command of English. The teachers spend a lot of time with them and my daughter is just not fully stretched. I've talked to the headmistress but she talks about our all having to live in a multicultural society and implies I'm racist. I'm not. My daughter's classmates are delightful but she isn't able to communicate with all of them and she's the one who is going to suffer.

A Of course you're not racist and it seems most unhelpful of the headmistress to resort to this argument when you have raised a legitimate problem and are genuinely concerned. The simple fact, however, is that if the school attended by your daughter is organized into classes of mixed ability (irrespective of race, colour or background), then there seems little you can do as long as your child remains at this school. If, however, the school does stream children according to their ability and attainment and you consider your daughter could be moved to a class more suited to her potential, then your first line of approach must be to her teachers and you can try to persuade the headmistress, through them, that your daughter is in the wrong class.

As a last resort, you could make enquiries of other schools in your local catchment area and if one suits, you could approach your local education authority and see if a place could be found for your daughter. This is difficult to accomplish but at least worth a try! Finally, if the local education authority can be shown to be failing to provide a place for your child appropriate to her age and ability, then the Secretary of State for Education can intervene. After all, there is a Parents' Charter now!

———

Q We came to Britain from Pakistan three years ago and are very happy except for one thing. Our seven-year-old is called names in the school playground. We think some of these children are guilty of racism and wonder how we can stop it.

A We sometimes think it would be a good idea if people coming to settle in Britain were given a crash course in understanding the natives and their sometimes perverse sense of humour! When we were at school, all jokes began: 'There was an Englishman, an Irishman, and a Scotsman' (never a Welshman for some reason!) and nicknames were the order of the day. 'Fats', 'Specky Four-Eyes', 'Carrots' and 'Skinny Lizzie' (who grew up to be an enviably slim model) were some of the repeatable ones; there was even a girl who was born in Germany and, although English, she was often greeted with 'Heil Hitler!'

Now it's not excusable but it's possible your child is not being treated any differently from anyone else. Why not find out? Why not get him to join in with a few nicknames of his own? You might have a word with his teacher but, beware! Being called 'Sneak' is worse than any other name children can dream up.

If you feel that the situation is not normal childhood name-calling and your child is really upset by this, then you can contact the school governors, the local education authority or even the Minister of Education's department with a view to removing your son to another school. It would be a pity if, in all other respects, he is happy and it is obviously difficult to regulate children's behaviour and attitudes entirely. (See also pp. 160, 210.)

————

Q My girlfriend became pregnant seven years ago. I immediately proposed and she accepted. Then, suddenly, she cancelled our wedding plans. She had our son, was given a council flat and I have paid child maintenance ever since. She would not allow me access to the child until three years ago. She likes to go out and is happy to hand him over almost every weekend. This is fine and I'm glad to say my son and I now have a wonderful relationship. However, once in a while, his mother will ring and say I can't see him that weekend. This is usually because she hasn't got a date, not because she wants to have Jamie. As you can imagine, Jamie gets very upset after he's been looking forward to seeing me and my sister's three children who are, after all, his cousins.

Could I now get access? Even if it were only one definite

weekend a month, it would be better for my son than this
'now you can/now you can't' attitude of his mother.

I have never defaulted on maintenance payments and for
the last three years I've taken Jamie away for a week's holiday.

A Access is now called 'contact'. You should seek advice
from a solicitor with a view to having a 'defined contact'
order from the court which you are entitled to do. Be warned,
however, if the mother flouts the arrangements there is, in
reality, *not* an enormous amount that the court can do since,
obviously, it is reluctant to commit any mother to prison.
However, you may feel more secure with a court order and
ultimately you might even want to extend your contact periods
and this would give a 'peg' on which to make such an application.

Q Our fifteen-year-old son has made an eighteen-year-old
girl pregnant. She led him on but I can't deny he is very
mature for his age. He is a very good student and we want
him to have a good career and life. But the girl says she
wants him to marry her when he is sixteen (in five months'
time). She makes veiled threats of what she will do if he
doesn't agree. We're worried sick. What is his legal position?
Could he be taken into care? And what about financial responsibility? We cannot support another child and our son has
years ahead of him before he gets a job. He doesn't want to
get married but accepts that he is the father. Is there any way
of establishing this for certain?

A Your very 'mature' son was unfortunate indeed to get
mixed up with a not very mature eighteen-year-old.
Clearly any marriage between these two would be a recipe for

disaster and your son should not be intimidated by threats. Indeed the young lady in question could find herself in trouble with the law for having had sexual intercourse with a boy under sixteen who is deemed to be too young to consent. Such conduct would be considered indecent assault on your son and viewed seriously. Unless your son is known to the authorities to be out of control and this incident is yet another example of his general conduct it seems unlikely that care proceedings will arise. As to financial responsibilities! Well, if a child is born, as the father he is as responsible as the mother, although he is technically the victim of a criminal act. An order for maintenance certainly cannot be made against you, as grandparents. If, in the unlikely event an order were made against him when he reaches sixteen years old, the amount will be determined according to his income which if this is NIL – well you cannot get blood out of a stone! And, after all, the lady in question can hardly have been unaware of her lover's financial position. Your son admits that he is the father but if he wishes to contest this when the child is born, he can challenge paternity and a test will be ordered. At the end of the day, your son has got himself into a pickle and it is to be hoped that the innocent child produced doesn't suffer the most. (See also p. 92.)

Q My ex-girlfriend is the mother of my five-year-old daughter, who I see on a regular basis. The mother has a boyfriend who, frankly, is not the kind of man I want around my child. His language is very bad and as a result my daughter sometimes uses words she shouldn't. Also, he drinks and I've a feeling he sometimes drives after he's had a few and I don't want my daughter in his car. Is there anything I can do about this? I'd be happy to have custody of my child but I'm wary of making waves in case my ex-girlfriend is deemed an unfit mother and the child is taken into care.

A The first thing is to get your ex-girlfriend alone for a non-combative chat about your child's welfare. Hopefully this will do the trick. If not, unless you and your girlfriend formally agree to share 'parental responsibility', your only legal recourse is to consider one of the options provided by the Children Act. You could apply for a contact order to include general periods of residence for your daughter at your home and you could apply for a full residence order (what used to be called care and control). It would not be impossible to regulate your child's contact with her mother's undesirable boyfriend but we would consider this very difficult and likely to cause further problems between you and the girl's mother.

Before taking any action involving possible court proceedings you ought to take advice from a solicitor specializing in child care cases.

Q During the holidays, my seven-year-old daughter's school operated a scheme of outings to various leisure centres for which we paid. Buses were laid on and we were assured the children would be supervised. However, after one such outing I learned that my daughter had been allowed to take herself across a busy road to a playground after she left the bus. I complained but was told that supervision did not include the time between leaving the bus and arriving at the centre. Can this be right? Supposing she had been knocked down?

A No, it cannot be right. As a parent participating in this scheme you had a right to expect responsible supervision at all times – including when roads had to be crossed! Thankfully, your daughter was not injured but, had she been, you would have had a strong claim against the organizers – probably the local authority responsible for the school. (See also pp. 65, 67.)

Q My husband and I are separated and I agreed that my eight-year-old son could stay for two weeks with his father during the summer holidays. I have just been told that he intends to go abroad with the child. I am so concerned about my son's welfare: he has never been away from me for longer than two days and I'm sure his father won't be able to cope. I shall be worried sick and helpless. Can I stop this even though my son wants to go with his father?

A If you have sound reasons for objecting to this trip based upon the welfare of the child – yes, you could well prevent this holiday. However, it sounds as though your natural maternal anxieties are at the root of your objections rather than any real possibility of a threat to your son's welfare. You should examine your motives very carefully before you take steps which could disappoint the child and even cause him to resent you. He isn't just 'your' son and it is in all your interests to have a good relationship with the boy's father, who seems to be taking his parental duties seriously. (See also p. 73.)

Q My son was divorced five years ago but my husband and I maintained a good relationship with his ex-wife and we continued to see and enjoy the company of our two grandchildren. Now we have been told that the children are likely to be taken to live in America as their mother is going to marry an American. Our son has consented to their going but we are distraught.

A We can imagine how devastating this news must be. Although the Children Act 1989 gives you the right to apply to intervene in the courts, the court could well permit this emigration if it is considered that it is in the children's best interests. And your son does agree, after all. Rather than acrimonious court proceedings, see if it is feasible for visits either way across the Atlantic to be arranged with your hitherto accommodating ex-daughter-in-law. (See also pp. 69, 71.)

Q My husband cannot take time off during the school holidays. We would like to take our children away during term-time but wonder what the position is. They are at a rather strict school and I'm slightly in awe of the headmistress myself so would like to have the facts at my fingertips.

A We're glad to hear there are some schools which care about education! In fact, you are quite within your rights to take your children away on holiday with you. But the regulations stress that, save in exceptional circumstances, only two weeks should be allowed in any one school year.

Q I have two small children and I live in terror of their knocking something off a shelf and breaking it whenever we're in a shop or store. My children are usually well behaved but some of the displays seem very precarious. What is the position if one of them accidentally breaks something? Would I have to pay?

A Sometimes a display is specifically marked, 'Please do not touch', and sometimes not, but if it is well stacked and properly visible then anyone breaking an item is liable to pay for it. A parent is likely to be responsible for a child picking something up and dropping it.

However, if a display is 'precarious', as you say, and can easily be knocked down then we consider that a customer can properly argue that the shop is at fault for failing to take reasonable measures to protect its goods.

Frankly, to save your having a nervous breakdown, we'd advise avoiding shops with fragile goods when you're out with the children. (See also p. 178.)

CHAPTER FIVE

MONEY MATTERS

I t was Benjamin Franklin who said, 'In this world nothing can be said to be certain, except death and taxes.' If you accept that (and we do), you've got a head start.

Taxes, along with other bills, invoices and demands for payment, can cause untold grief if you don't get a grip on your financial affairs. Always ask for a receipt, read the small print on every document and don't be afraid to ask questions – you should always be sure you know what you're signing.

As for death, our advice is not to be like Mr Micawber, always waiting for something to turn up. We've seen too many long-lost, unwelcome relatives turn up at the prospect of any money. You can have some influence after your death if you make your will – and make it NOW!

———

Q I am worried because my husband refuses to make a will. He says that I would get everything when he dies and I would have no problems. We have two young children and my husband has a child from a previous marriage. Is he right?

A Where there is no will, the surviving spouse is now entitled to the first £125,000 of the deceased's estate. So your husband would be right if, on his death, he left assets not exceeding that amount. Once the estate goes above £125,000 then all the children, including those of a former marriage, are entitled to their half share of the remaining portion of the estate. You would not, therefore, inherit everything if your husband is likely to leave assets which are in excess of £125,000 in England. In Scotland, the rules of intestacy work slightly differently with entitlement to land, furniture and other items in the estate being valued and apportioned. Our strong advice wherever you live is to make a will, however few assets you may have. (See also pp. 94, 95.)

Q My aunt died recently aged seventy-nine. She had two sons and a daughter, none of whom visited her until her final illness. I lived nearby and popped in most days to see her. She had always complained about her children and said she was leaving everything to me. Over the years she gave me odd pieces of jewellery, including her beautiful diamond engagement ring. She died intestate, however, so I think the money will go to her children, who are already arguing among themselves. What upsets me is not the money but the fact that her oldest son says he wants the engagement ring back. He has virtually accused me of getting it from her while she was ill and says it was promised to him for his wife. It isn't true. What can I do? I'd like the ring as a memento because I loved the old lady dearly.

A As your aunt gave you the ring while she was alive, you are entitled to keep it as it does not form part of her estate. If her greedy son contests your entitlement, he will have to prove that you exercised undue influence over his mother which led to her giving you the jewellery. Given the facts stated, it is doubtful that he would take action, let alone succeed. (See also pp. 88, 93.)

Q My great-aunt has died and left me an annual week's time-share in a place I do not like. Do I have to accept it? I neither want it nor the trouble of getting rid of it.

A Most people grin and bear it when they're left an obnoxious pet poodle or a particularly ugly dinner set but they don't have to. Any beneficiary can refuse anything they do not want. If you are informed of an unwelcome bequest, simply write to the solicitor concerned and refuse it.

As to what then happens to the unwanted cat or cutlery, the executor of the will can sell the item and put the proceeds into the residue of the estate (i.e. what is left over after all bequests have been dealt with); if the item cannot be sold, e.g. a cat, it can be given away.

Q After thirty years, I have traced my father. I am his illegitimate daughter and my mother registered me as the daughter of the man she married before I was born. My father has a daughter by his marriage prior to my birth. Although I have no proof except my mother's word, my real father does accept me as his daughter. What I would like to know is, if my father were to die leaving no will, can I make any claim on his estate?

A You most certainly can! Since 1969, an illegitimate child has the same rights on the intestacy of a parent as if they were legitimate. Indeed, even if your father were to leave a will in which he referred only to his 'children', you would be included in that reference. If, as you say, your father accepts and looks upon you as his daughter then you might even be entitled to reasonable provision from his estate notwithstanding a will from which you were excluded, but that has to be dependent upon the exact nature of your ongoing relationship and your needs, if any, at the time of his death. However, in the event of conflict over the estate, you must be able to satisfy a court that you are indeed your father's daughter. (See also p. 6.)

Q My father is eighty and lives alone. He's fiercely independent but he is becoming increasingly forgetful. Sometimes I find gas and electricity bills that are long overdue for payment. I'm afraid he might be cut off and have to pay to be reconnected, not to mention having to manage without these services in the interim. Is it possible for me to sign cheques on his behalf?

A No. But your father can grant you a power of attorney or, in Scotland, a deed of factory and commission, which allows you to take over the management of his money when he cannot do it himself. Where available, you can use a special form called an 'Enduring Power of Attorney', which is available from law stationers or from the Oyez Stationery Group, 159 Bermondsey Street, London SE1 4PU. The form isn't a very easy one, so you might want the help of a solicitor in drawing it up. Your father has to be fully aware of what he is doing when he grants you power of attorney, otherwise it will be invalid.

For information leaflets on enduring powers of attorney, write to Public Trust Office, Protection Division, Stewart House, Kingsway, London WC2B 6JX.

———

Q My widower father has died, leaving the majority of his estate to me and my brother. But my brother was killed in a crash just two days before my father's death. Do I now inherit everything or do I have to share with my deceased brother's wife and their three children?

A Your position under your late father's will remains unaffected as your brother's share now passes directly to his children. Generally, if a beneficiary named in a will dies before the maker of the will, the legacy lapses and becomes part of the residue of the estate of the will maker. However, as in your case, where children or grandchildren are named beneficiaries and they die first, their share passes on, in turn, to their children, if any. Your late brother's children now stand in the shoes of their father and together with you will inherit under their grandfather's will.

———

Q In my pay packet last week I discovered that twice my usual wages had been put in although my pay slip was for the normal amount due. As this was clearly paid by mistake I returned the extra to my employers, but would I have been entitled to keep it as I had received it innocently?

A Your receipt of the extra money was innocent but once the mistake was discovered and you realized that you were not entitled to it, then any retention of the money would have been theft and you were right to have returned it. We trust your employers fully appreciate your honesty and integrity! (See also pp. 119, 212.)

Q I was left some antique furniture by an elderly aunt. Our house is modern and a local antiques dealer offered to have the furniture in his shop with a view to selling it for me. We then went on our annual holiday and on our return found the shop closed down. Enquiries revealed that the shop and all its contents were in the hands of receivers. What about my furniture?

A Contact the receivers and explain that you own the furniture. It is not and never was part of the stock to be taken into account for the shop's creditors. You are entitled to the return of your property or its full value without delay.

Q I lost my engagement ring but when I made a claim, I discovered that the ring was not insured because the broker had forgotten to forward my premium to the insurance company. Surely the company is responsible for the actions of the broker who supplies them with insurance business?

A No! The insurance broker is your agent and responsible to you – not the insurance company. If the insurers refuse to meet your claim, you must sue your incompetent broker. (See also p. 97.)

Q My husband and I divorced last year and he went to live with his mother and stepfather, whilst our three young children live with me. Who is his next-of-kin if he dies and where do my children stand if he remarries?

A Your children are your ex-husband's next-of-kin. If he remarries and has other children, they, too, will be his next-of-kin, as will his new wife if she survives him.

———

Q Our elderly disabled neighbour has relied upon me for years to help her in her daily chores and needs. She has recently said that she intends to leave me everything in her will. If she makes this generous gesture, could the will be challenged by long-lost relatives?

A Such relatives inevitably appear from the woodwork when money is involved, but if your neighbour is encouraged to seek independent legal advice when the will is drawn up, it will be difficult for anyone to say that you have exercised unfair influence over her. (See also pp. 84, 93.)

———

Q I was divorced twenty-three years ago and brought up my two daughters. My ex-husband remarried twice although when he died last year, he was a widower. I have never married again. My ex-husband left no will and I want to know if I or my daughters have any claim on his estate.

A Your daughters certainly have a claim. You will have no claim unless you had depended on him for maintenance all these years, in which event you could be entitled to something. We must stress the importance of making a will. Had your ex-husband's last wife survived him and/or if he had had more children, his affairs would be very difficult to sort out.

———

Q I'm worried because I have not received a bill for water rates for four years. I've heard nothing from any water authority and I'm afraid that a bill could come anytime demanding payment in full, which I couldn't afford to pay.

A We had a similar experience with an electricity bill! Although it's tempting to leave it, it's best for you to make the first move: contact the water company office and when the amount due is sorted out, insist on being permitted to pay over a time and at a rate that you can afford. It's their mistake; they are sure to accommodate you.

———

Q I am soon to remarry but my fiancé has far less to put into a joint property than I have. How can I make sure that my two children inherit my share of the property or will my fiancé and I automatically own it fifty-fifty, regardless of our contributions? I have made a will leaving all my money to my children. Is that good enough?

A It's very sensible to sort these matters out before you marry and the answer is, no, it is not enough to rely upon a will that is likely to become invalid when you marry. You must ensure that your share in the new house remains separately owned by you. This is called a 'tenancy in common'. Your solicitor can easily arrange this, and you can then leave your property to whom you please. (See also pp. 49, 92, 96, 105.)

———

Q I am interested to know the contents of a distant cousin's will. Is it possible to obtain a copy of the will of a deceased person?

A If the will has been admitted to probate, that is, the
process which starts the administration of the deceased's
estate, you can obtain a copy from Somerset House, The
Strand, London, WC2A 2U; Tel: 0171 936 7000. As long as
you have the full name and date of death, a copy will be made
for you although a small fee will be charged for this service.

———

Q My son sold his car to a man who paid with a building
society cheque. He soon discovered the cheque was
worthless as it was part of a stolen batch. My son's insurance
company doesn't want to know and both the buyer and the
car have disappeared. Is there anything that he can do?

———

A He can go straight back to his insurers. Your son's car
was 'stolen' in accordance with court cases decided on
similar facts. Since the car was insured against theft, your
son's insurers are obliged to pay out. (See also pp. 99, 101,
188, 192.)

———

Q My first marriage ended in 1985 when I left my husband
in the matrimonial home which was in joint names. I
married again but the house remained unsold and my ex-
husband still lives there. No court order has ever been made
and now I want to ensure that my interest is transferred to
my children. What should I do? I do not even know what my
entitlement is.

———

A You should consult a solicitor with a view to having a
simple declaration of trust drawn up by deed. This will
pass whatever interest you presently have to whomever you
nominate. Your solicitor can check the land register to find
out what your legal interest is.

Q I have been living with my boyfriend for just over three years. We are buying a house and it is in our joint names. Six months ago, his mother and father asked me to be a witness to their will – which I agreed to. Now I am worried that my boyfriend will lose his legacy and everything will go to his two brothers – one of whom has been left only a small sum of money; the rest of his parents' belongings are to be split between my boyfriend and the other brother. We intend to marry within the next two years.

A Your concern is understandable but do be reassured that your relationship with your boyfriend will not affect his entitlement under his parents' will and neither will your marriage to him at a later stage. It has been settled law for more than 100 years that where a will has been executed, the subsequent marriage between a beneficiary and a witness to the will does not affect the provisions of the will.

Q Are we responsible for our son's debts? He is an eighteen-year-old student and is heavily overdrawn at the bank.

A Some of those bank advertisements have a lot to answer for! Teenagers become seduced into getting themselves in over their heads and mums and dads are then called upon to bail them out! However, you have no legal obligation to discharge your son's debts. He is over the age of majority and responsible for himself. Unless you have agreed with the bank to be a guarantor of your son's overdraft debt, the bank cannot look to you, simply as a parent, to make good the money owed by their customer, your son. (See also p. 77.)

Q I hope this doesn't sound too mean but I am the youngest of three sisters. The eldest has had no contact with the family for years, choosing to ignore all of us, including our father who died a short time ago. Although our father made a will leaving everything to all three of us in equal shares, he did alter the will by crossing out my eldest sister's name and initialling the alteration, intending only myself and my middle sister to benefit. We have been told that this alteration does not have legal effect and the will is to stand as originally drafted. Is this right? And does it make any difference that the will had been altered at the offices of my father's solicitor and apparently, with his approval.

A It is indeed right that such an alteration will have no legal effect in England. To alter a will as your father wished, there should have been a new document drawn, called a codicil or, better still, a fresh will made. However, if the attempted alteration was made while your father was receiving the 'benefit' of legal advice from his solicitor, then the solicitor ought to have known better. He could well be liable to you and your middle sister for your losses under the will because your eldest sister is now taking the share that your father finally intended her not to have. You should put this matter into the hands of a *competent* solicitor. In Scotland, such an alteration might well be effective if it is authenticated. (See also pp. 49, 89, 96, 98, 105.)

––––––

Q My father died two years ago and left our home jointly to my elderly mother and me. I am an only child and expect to inherit the remaining half of the property from my mother together with the remainder of my parents' estate. However, my mother has befriended a young neighbour who is turning her against me and I now believe that this young woman may be influencing my mother to change her will in favour of herself and her children. Do I have any redress if I find this is, in fact, the case?

A If on her death you find that your mother had changed her will in favour of this neighbour, you might well be able to challenge it. Firstly, the court would have to be satisfied that your mother was of sound mind when her last will was made. Then the serious issue of undue influence on the part of this young woman could be considered. Finally, you might successfully claim under the Inheritance (Provision for Family and Dependents) Act 1975 that you have not been given reasonable provision under your mother's will. You should seek the services of a competent solicitor should your worst fears be realized. However, why not discuss this with your mother? She might tell you that you have no grounds for your worries. (See also pp. 84, 88.)

Q I ordered some goods from a mail order company whose order form I cut out from their small catalogue. The price I paid included an insurance charge of thirty pence but the goods have never arrived. Unfortunately, the order form contained the company address and, of course, I no longer have this and it appears nowhere else in the catalogue. How do I stand with the insurance?

A Well, of course, if you trace the insurers then you would be able to trace the company and demand to know the whereabouts of your goods. It is difficult to advise on your insurance position without knowing the terms upon which cover was effected and, indeed, whether it was effected at all.

You must try to trace the company by seeing if you can get hold of another catalogue, scouring the newspapers for further company offers or even, if the company is limited and you can recall its full name, you might consider it worthwhile to contact Companies House, to request a company search which would give you the address.

———

Q My husband and I are pensioners and we have our home and all our savings in joint names. When we both die, we intend the whole of our estate to be divided equally between our two married children. Is there any advantage or purpose in our making wills as, on the first death, the remaining partner will automatically inherit the whole estate? Is it not enough to make a will when only one of us is left?

A Generally, it is sensible for each of you to make a will but if all of your estate is jointly owned then the survivor will automatically inherit everything and this is one situation where we agree that there seems no need for a will to be drawn up until one of you has passed away. We strongly recommend a will be made at that stage since it is always easier to deal with an estate under a will than under intestacy.

Consider though, however unlikely it might seem, that you might both die at the same time – in a car crash, for instance. It would be terrible if the grief of your children were compounded by problems with inheritance. (See also p. 83.)

———

Q Can you please tell me who will benefit from an estate where the deceased was a bachelor and whose only surviving family are two brothers and two sisters? Is the estate shared equally or does it all go to the eldest brother or sister?

A In the case of an intestacy where there are only surviving brothers or sisters, the estate is divided equally between them with no distinction being made as to their seniority. (See also p. 83.)

———

Q I am a widow with two married daughters and three grandchildren. I have a house and some money which I want to divide so that the grandchildren will each have something and also a niece and nephew of whom I am very fond. I feel that what I want to do is simple enough not to need a solicitor and I can draw up my own will. Do you think that I am unwise and should I seek legal help?

A If you feel that your wishes are quite straightforward and your estate fairly simple to sort out, then you ought to be able to make your own will. There are printed forms, obtainable from stationers such as Oyez, which can guide you. Certain fundamental points have to be followed though and these are: the will must be in writing and stated to be your last will; you must make sure that all your property and money is disposed of in the will; you must clearly identify the persons benefiting from your will (the beneficiaries) and you should make sure that at least two persons (as you are leaving property) are named as executors to deal with the estate. The executors can be beneficiaries unlike the witnesses (at least two), who must see you and each other sign the will on completion. Finally, if you want to change anything after the will is drafted, you cannot simply cross out and alter the writing. You must either draft a whole new document or draw up a small addition to the will – called a codicil – which must be signed and witnessed formally. If you have any real doubts about whether you can draw up a will yourself, you are well advised to see a solicitor. It does rather defeat the point if you think you have saved expense by doing it yourself but then the whole estate is eaten up in legal fees to sort it out afterwards. (See also pp. 49, 89, 92, 98, 105.)

————

Q My husband and I took out an insurance policy to cover the contents of our house. Following a burglary we now discover that we were 'underinsured', which means that we don't get back from the insurers all of our losses. We took advice from an insurance broker, who assured us that we were fully covered and even helped us fill in the proposal form. The insurance company refuses to budge, however, and now it seems that after the distress of our home being broken into, we can't even be fully compensated! What exactly does being 'underinsured' mean? We are not, after all, claiming the loss of all the contents.

A When you are said to be 'underinsured', this means that the full value of your contents was not covered. Therefore, when you make a claim on this contents policy you can only receive the same proportion of your claim as is represented by your insurance cover: for example, if you are underinsured by one-third of the true value of your house contents, the insurers are entitled to deduct one-third from your claim to them. It's worth remembering that when you rely upon an insurance broker or agent, he normally acts on your behalf and not on behalf of the insurance company. Therefore, if, as seems to be the case here, you received wrong advice, the insurance company is not liable. If, however, the broker is worth suing, you would probably have a remedy against him and if, indeed, your failure to receive full compensation was proved to be caused by following his 'advice', you should be able to make up your losses from him. It is all a matter of proportion. (See also p. 87.)

––––––

Q I renewed my insurance cover for two rings a few months ago then lost one of the rings. I have claimed from the insurance company but they have refused to pay me out as they say I did not tell them that my husband had a conviction for dishonesty in the past year! Surely what my husband does should not affect me? The policy was in my name and I have always paid it.

A It is a tough decision and one perhaps worth pressing with the insurance company but, legally, they are entitled to take advantage of any fact that might be regarded as 'material to the policy', which has not been disclosed to them. Even if you cannot see the importance or relevance of certain facts, you are under an obligation to provide full and frank details of anything which might affect the insurance company's attitude. Otherwise, they invariably have an 'out' in accordance with the small print of the policy. It is essential to read the policy document carefully and, if in any doubt, to provide the information or seek assistance from the insurance company itself. (See also p. 179.)

––––––

Q I have been married and divorced twice and for the past ten years have lived happily with my lover. He is divorced. Neither of us has any children but he has a sister and three nieces on whom he dotes. He tells me that in his will he has left me the house we live in (it's his and in his name). I'm perfectly happy to continue as we are as I've not exactly been an advertisement for happy marriage, but a friend of mine has been sowing seeds of doubt in my mind. I'm not a gold-digger and I don't want to be whatever you call an unmarried widow, but I would like to feel secure that the house is definitely mine. I have no doubts that the house has been left to me but could his family have any claims on it? They have, incidentally, been provided for in the will. The point my friend makes is that unmarried people just do not have the same rights as a spouse, however long and close the relationship and whatever the terms of a will. Is this so? I would like to know any snags in continuing as I am now.

A We hope you won't be an 'unmarried widow' (we can't think of a good word for it, either) for many years to come. But we would stress to you and to married people as well – which means everyone – the importance of making a will and getting all arrangements sorted out. It's not a question of being a gold-digger. It's a matter of sensible planning, just as you'd plan a holiday or organize a mortgage or think about your job prospects. It is a fact that a widow might be in a stronger position to resist any claim by other members of the family who might seek to upset the terms of a will. However, the size of the estate, the relationship of all parties, including yourself, to the deceased, your means, the assets of the other relatives and their expectations are all matters which have to be considered in the event of any claim being made. (See also pp. 49, 92, 96, 105.)

Q I left my car for an hour and when I got back to it, found that personal belongings, including my camera had been taken. If I claim for this theft, will I lose my no-claims bonus?

A It varies from insurance company to insurance company so you must check with your insurers and look carefully at the terms of your policy. Even if, strictly, your no-claims bonus could be affected by making a claim, your insurance company has a discretion in the matter if it considers you to have been completely blameless. (See also pp. 90, 101, 188.)

———

Q My father has died and I find he has left substantial debts on three credit cards. Must these be paid out of his estate?

A Yes. Credit card debts are the same as any other debts outstanding when a person dies and must be settled in the same way.

———

Q My husband and I found a flat which we liked and we felt we could just afford to buy. We made an offer which was accepted, instructed solicitors, obtained an offer of a mortgage and sent a surveyor for a check. Imagine our disappointment and frustration when we discovered that the owner of the flat had sold to another couple at a higher price! Now we find that we have a bill from both the solicitors and the surveyor. Is there any way we can claim these expenses from the owner? After all, he led us to believe that the flat was ours.

A What you have described is the classic case of gazumping in England and Wales, a disgraceful practice that is unfortunately so common that the word now appears in the dictionary. It adds insult to injury to be let down in this way and then face legal and other bills on top. Unfortunately, when you agree to buy a property in England and Wales, you have no legal relationship with the seller until contracts are actually exchanged – hence the phrase 'subject to contract' whenever property is offered for sale. We would love to say otherwise, but the only possibility that exists of the vendor being responsible for legal and other costs if he pulls out at the last minute is if this is negotiated as part of the initial agreement when your offer is accepted but before full contracts are signed and exchanged. In Scotland, however, there is a greater measure of protection for both buyer and seller. If a firm, written offer is made for a property and is accepted unconditionally in a prescribed written form, then neither party can opt out of the agreement simply because the price, after all, doesn't suit either one of them.

———

Q I rent my flat, which is one of a number in a small block. I and the other tenants heard that the landlord who owns the block was negotiating to sell it and we have met together and decided that as a group, we would like to buy his interest. We approached the landlord but have met with no response. Surely this landlord cannot sell above our heads if we have shown that we wish to be considered as purchasers? If he does sell to an outside party, is there anything we could do?

A If your landlord does sell to an outside party, he could well be in breach of a fairly new law which allows tenants far greater rights than they previously had. The Landlord and Tenant Act 1987 (England and Wales) gives tenants in your position a first option to buy their landlord's interest, assuming proper terms and conditions can be agreed. If the landlord fails to offer his interest to the tenants and sells elsewhere, they can require the purchaser to resell the interest on the terms on which he bought. As with all matters affecting property, you should seek professional guidance on how the legislation works, which parts of the Act are actually in force and, just as important, the best way of securing a good deal for all of you if the law permits and you decide to assert your rights to buy. (See also pp. 39, 40, 41, 44, 45, 51.)

———

Q As my husband was coming down the stairs carrying a pot of paint (bright yellow, unfortunately), he tripped and the paint went all over the stair carpet and also on to his trousers. He wasn't decorating at the time, just transporting the paint from upstairs to the kitchen. Try as we have, we cannot remove the stains. I have a new-for-old household contents policy. Can I claim on it?

A The small print of your insurance policy will tell you whether you can claim successfully for your newly painted carpet and trousers or whether you will have to live with partially bright yellow stairs, passing them off as 'art nouveau'! Only if your policy gives you full accidental damage cover will you be able to claim. Most household policies give only limited protection for television, video and glass damage and this would not be enough to restore carpets or trousers to their former glory. (See also pp. 90, 99, 188.)

———

Q I was away for the weekend a couple of months ago and my flat was broken into and burgled. I sorted things out with my insurers but now my telephone bill has come and I'm horrified to see that it's about £250 more than usual. When I checked, I discovered that, on the weekend in question, calls were made from my flat to America and Australia and heaven knows where else. I explained this to British Telecom but they say that I have to pay and if I don't, I'll be cut off and have to pay a reconnection charge if I want the phone restored. The police have not caught the burglars. Will I really have to pay this bill? I don't have that kind of money to spare but I do need a telephone.

A It adds insult to injury to discover that not only has your home been violated but the burglars also took time to make several calls overseas – at your expense. Regrettably, there is little you can do but pay up if you want to hang on to your telephone. Check back with your insurers but we doubt that you will be covered for this loss. However, you might think it worth telling the police. If British Telecom has a record of the calls, they might also have a record of the numbers called. The police might be able to find out who received the calls and, from them, the identity of the caller.

Q My parents run a newsagent's and stationery shop and a customer has defaulted on a long-running stationery account, leaving a debt of over £200. He admits the debt but refuses to pay up, saying that it was his company's liability and the company has gone into liquidation. My parents can ill afford to sustain this loss and wonder whether they have a claim against him. The account was in his name and, although he did pay some bills on a company cheque, they did not realize they were dealing with a company.

A Oh dear – your parents are the victims of an all too common dodge by unscrupulous debtors. If they were led to believe that they were supplying an individual at all times and the account was in a personal name as you say, then there is every reason to suppose that they can proceed against their customer for the money despite what he says.

The fact that a company cheque was sometimes used to pay bills should make no difference whatsoever and may merely indicate that the customer chose to use a company bank account to pay his own bills.

———

Q I had an accident in 1983. A writ was issued in the High Court in 1986 and the case has been prepared for trial but no date has yet been given for the case to be heard. I've been in contact with my solicitors but cannot get satisfaction from them and my patience is exhausted. Is there any reason why I should not go to another solicitor even though I am on legal aid? Also, how do I know if my legal aid is still valid?

A It seems a pity that your case cannot now be heard without going to the trouble of changing your solicitors. However, if your present solicitors seem reluctant to keep you fully informed as to the progress of your case, there is nothing to prevent you from instructing a new firm of solicitors and your file will be passed to them. Before taking this step, we would advise you to insist on an appointment with your present solicitors to air your concerns fully and find out about your legal aid position. You can then decide whether to stay where you are or change to a new firm. But you should act quickly – enough time has been wasted already and the courts nowadays take a dim view of 'stale' cases. (See also pp. 109, 125.)

———

Q I lent my friend a very special and expensive blouse. The waiter spilled soup on it and it left a nasty stain. She had it cleaned but the stain hasn't come out completely. She can't afford to replace it but neither can I. Is there anything I can do? Should the hotel pay up? I'm afraid my friend and I are barely on speaking terms now.

A To ensure long-lasting friendships – don't sell your car to a friend and don't lend good clothes! However, in this case, the hotel ought certainly to pay up. Waiters are not expected to throw things over guests except in comedy sketches and the hotel management is liable to you for the negligence of its staff.

––––––

Q My husband has left me and I've just discovered that he's wiped out the content of our joint account. It contained a lot of money as we both have high disposable incomes. Can I get my share back?

A You can sue your husband for the return of your share of the account since he is not entitled to spend your part of the money without accounting to you for it. However, this could cost more money than you had, so if you can frighten him with this information into repaying what he owes, so much the better. (See also p. 10.)

––––––

Q I was a widow with two children (now twenty-five and twenty-four, married with children of their own) when I met my present husband six years ago. We live in the house my first husband left me but my husband pays all the bills and has also bought a small cottage in the country. He had not been married before and says he is leaving everything to me. What worries me is whether this means I must leave everything to him? Although I love him dearly, if I were to die first, he would have his cottage and enough to live on. I would like to leave the bulk of my estate to my children.

I can't see it happening but I know that inheritances can set people at each other's throats; so, if my husband did want to claim my estate, could he do so?

A You're right about inheritance causing trouble among the seemingly most close families but in your case there should be no problem. You can leave your worldly goods to whomsoever you please and any challenge to your wishes will only succeed if you have failed to provide reasonable provision for someone who could have expected support from you.

In your case, your husband, though paying all the bills, has had the benefit of living in your property and has been able to use his capital to buy the cottage. He would seemingly be reasonably provided for if your children had the benefit of your estate and there would seem little prospect of succeeding in any challenge to your will. But do make that will. (See also pp. 49, 89, 92, 96.)

———

Q Before splitting up with my boyfriend, we went on a two-week holiday in Tenerife. As he was unemployed at the time but about to start a new job, I agreed to lend him the money to pay his share of the holiday expenses which amounted to around £350. Obviously, I now want the money back, but he refuses to pay it in a lump sum, insisting he pay it at £10 a month because, he says, he is hard up. I know that he is earning more than I am now and don't see why he should get away with this. What do you suggest?

A Well, you could take action against him and obtain a county court judgment for the full amount. Be warned, however, he will probably plead hardship to the court, who could very well be persuaded to permit him to pay you off at £10 per month – so you would be back to square one.

———

Q I'm the single mother of a three-year-old boy. At the time he was conceived, I was living with a boyfriend. I was beginning to tire of the relationship and had had a couple of one-night stands. To be honest, I don't really know who the father is but my old boyfriend thinks he is. I didn't want to marry him and I was given a council flat. I was also awarded £10 a week from my boyfriend who stated he was the father. I didn't want him to have access to my son and the court upheld this. Now he's sent a message via a friend to say he's getting fed up and is going to apply for a blood test to be taken to determine paternity. I'm so afraid. Can he insist on this and if it's found he's not the father, will I have to pay back the money I've had from him to date?

A Since you appear to have had a court award you maintenance for your child, it is likely that your ex-boyfriend was adjudged to be the father. If he wanted to challenge this finding, he would normally have twenty-one days in which to do it but the court which hears the appeal from the order can extend the period and can order blood tests if they consider that there are proper grounds for doing so. You don't have to cooperate with any blood test order but if you take that line the court can draw conclusions against you. If your ex-boyfriend's appeal were made within the twenty-one day period and successful, you could be ordered to repay monies received. If he appeals successfully at a much later date, the court would be unlikely to order you to repay the money unless you could easily afford to do so or if it was found that the original order was made as a consequence of deliberate deception on your part. (See also pp. 14, 108.)

Q My son attends a school where rugby is compulsory. I read recently that there are several thousand accidents on school sports fields each year, some of them very serious. It set me thinking what the legal situation is if a child is injured while playing sports at school. Who is responsible and is it possible to claim compensation?

A Accidents at school are indeed more frequent than one might suppose but a school authority is not generally insured for all accidental injury. If negligence or incompetence result in injury in the school playground, science lab or on the rugby field, then the school will be responsible and its insurers will probably pick up the appropriate tab. Otherwise, you should check with the school as to whether there happens to be accident insurance in force and, if not, and if you are worried, you should consider taking out a policy yourself. (See also pp. 65, 67.)

Q My boyfriend's ex-fiancée is pregnant and although he has her on tape saying that the baby is not his, he is quite sure it is. She told him she doesn't want him to see the baby when it's born and he says that, this being the case, he will not have to pay maintenance. Is this true? If she does want maintenance, would the tape stand up in court? If he does have to pay maintenance, will the court take into account hire purchase agreements he has when they make their decision on how much he will have to pay? Also, if she decides not to claim maintenance now but changes her mind when the baby is older – can she still claim it?

A You certainly have a lot of questions! Does your boyfriend ever get a word in edgeways!

Even if your boyfriend does not see the child, it does not mean that he might not be ordered to pay maintenance if the court rules that the child was his. However, the mother would have to apply within three years of the birth and the tape would certainly be allowed in court, although it would not be conclusive. Your boyfriend's financial obligations would then be fully considered and it is the Child Support Agency which would decide the size of your boyfriend's obligations. However, the mother can apply at any future date if your boyfriend were to provide money or gifts for the child up to its third birthday, thus implying that he accepts parternity and, therefore, responsibility. (See also pp. 14, 107.)

Q Six years ago, my son went into hospital for a routine operation. Because of negligence, he came out severely brain-damaged. He requires constant attention as he now has the mental age of a six-year-old (he's eighteen). We sued the medical authorities and our solicitor advised us to accept the £8,000 offer of compensation. As you can imagine, the money has long since been swallowed up. At a local meeting of parents of disabled children last week, I met a woman who had undergone a similar experience. But she had been awarded £105,000. She told me I had obviously picked the wrong solicitor. But how do you get the right one for your case? And can I take any action against the man who advised me to settle for so little?

A It is impossible to know who is or is not the right lawyer for the job but some firms of solicitors specialize in different fields and medical negligence is one. It would have been worth finding a specialist firm by either making enquiries amongst the very group you belong to, or directly to the Law Society, 113 Chancery Lane, London WC2 1PA.

As to whether the compensation you received was adequate, this depends upon the facts of the case and whether you could prove negligence. If you could, or if negligence were admitted, then you could well have a claim against your solicitor for wrong advice. The claim would be brought in the name of your son. Because he is now eighteen years old but with a young mental age, this would probably require the inter-vention of the Official Solicitor (curator in Scotland). In the first instance, find a specialist firm who will advise you on the chances of success and the complicated procedure for bringing a claim against your former solicitor. (See also pp. 104, 125.)

Q Six months after buying my car it was written off in an accident (not my fault). My insurers have offered me £600 less than I paid for it which, after paying the finance company, leaves me in difficulty to buy another car. Can I challenge their offer?

A You can try to negotiate but your insurers' obligation is to pay you only the present market value of your car which could well be what has been offered even though you, the innocent party, end up with what seems a raw deal.

Q My friends and I send in our football pools coupons through our local newsagent, paying him the stake money. What happens if he fails to deliver our coupon? As he is an official agent, can we sue the pools company if we happened to win?

A It would appear not. Pools agents are agents for the clients, that is punters like yourselves. This means you would have no case against the pools company, although you might have one against the agent. In the awful event of a winning coupon not being delivered, you might consider consulting a solicitor to see if it is worth pursuing your losses against the agent. One factor will be whether he is able to meet any claim brought against him.

———

Q I was adopted by my maternal grandparents when I was three years old, following the divorce of my parents. I found out that my real father is a very wealthy man although I have had no contact with him since my adoption. I also discovered that my father remarried but had no other children. I now have an adult son of my own and I want to know whether he or I could have any claim on my father's estate and, if necessary, could contest any will that he might make.

A Once a legal adoption has taken place, the adopted child is treated in law as the child of the adopters and no one else. Thus it seems that neither you nor your son have any legal claim on your father's estate or right to contest his will. If, however, you wish to contact your father for personal reasons or if an adopted person, on reaching eighteen, wishes to make contact with their real parents but has no knowledge of the parents' whereabouts or even identity, a call to the British Agencies of Adoption and Fostering on 0171–593 2000 or to the Salvation Army will put you on the right track.

――――

Q I saw a lovely garden furniture set in a department store which announced interest-free credit. I decided to pay for it in easy monthly instalments. However, I was turned down. I've been trying to find out what the problem is but I can't get any satisfaction. I seem to be on some sort of credit blacklist but, although I've bought lots of things on hire purchase in the past, I've never been in arrears or defaulted on payment. How can I find out what has happened?

A This store, or indeed any organization which offers credit, is not legally obliged to tell you why you have been refused credit but there is a good chance that a refusal has been based upon information received by them from a credit reference agency.

You can demand to know which credit reference agency has supplied the information about your credit standing and they are obliged to give you the name and address within twenty-eight days of your application to buy the furniture on credit. You should then write to the agency who, in turn, must supply you with a copy of your recorded details and may charge a small fee. If no details are known, the agency must tell you that also.

The credit reference agency holds information ranging from a record of subscribers who have requested credit details about you, together with transactions in which you have been involved with your prior record of repayment, to any out-standing county court judgments. In Scotland, decrees replace judgments. If you do not agree with the information recorded under your name, you can require the agency to remove or

111

amend its records, stating your reasons in full, and the agency is bound by law to respond within twenty-eight days. If the agency fails to respond or amend its records, you can send a 'Notice of Correction', which should be a clear explanation of why you believe the entry needs altering. Your local citizen's advice bureau can help you draft the note if necessary. The note then has to be added to the file. However, this is not the end of the story if you are still not satisfied. You are further entitled, under the Consumer Credit Act 1974, to write to the Director General of Fair Trading, Field House, Bream's Buildings, London EC4A 1PR, setting out your grievances over the incorrect entry. This office will contact the agency on your behalf and investigate your complaint.

If you see or believe there is a judgment or decree entered against you and if this has now been satisfied, you are well advised to apply to the court concerned for a 'Certificate of Satisfaction', which for a £1 fee will be issued by the Public Registry and will result in the removal from public records of any unpaid judgment. A copy of this will be sent to the credit reference agencies who will record that judgment has been satisfied. In Scotland, there is no equivalent procedure for the registration of 'satisfaction' as just described but if you can provide suitable evidence that payment has been made, your file will indicate that the decree has been paid.

Finally, if you want to make a general enquiry as to your credit standing, we have listed several credit data agencies at the end of the book to whom you can write.

If you wish to make sure that all national records relating to your creditworthiness are accurate, you should contact Registry Trust Limited, 173–175 Cleveland Street, London W1P 5PE.

———

Q I was dashing through the rain, head down, umbrella up and I crashed straight into someone coming towards me. The point of my umbrella just missed the man's eye but it set me thinking. What happens if you cause someone an injury in a case like this? And is there any kind of insurance you can take out to cover such a contingency?

A Yes, and it makes sense to consider a private liability insurance policy, which would cover the kind of situation you have outlined. You can take out legal insurance to cover the possibility of being sued which would cover you for legal fees and other costs. We feel that either one of these policies would be a sensible precaution.

———

Q My youngest son works for a bank. He persuaded me to let him invest my savings for me. I have now discovered that he invested my savings in his own name and he has now withdrawn and used all my money. I am shocked and hurt but without proof that the money was mine. Can I do anything at all to get it back?

A This is a terrible thing to happen. Your son has abused your trust and acted dishonestly. He has converted your money to his own use and to try to get it back could be a painful and distressing experience. It will be your word against his that the money was not a gift to him. You should see a solicitor or even consider involving the police.

May we stress that, whether dealing with close family or strangers, it avoids trouble in the long run if you put any transaction in writing.

———

113

Q On my return from holiday, I immediately sent off the amount due on my credit card demand which had arrived in my absence. Unfortunately, by the time I was able to send it, it arrived one day after the due date on the demand. I was then disgusted to discover that I had been charged a full month's interest on the whole amount which was only one day late! Can the credit card companies really get away with this?

A They can and frequently do! Their terms and conditions entitle them to charge the full rate for any late payment. We can only advise that you create a fuss and try to persuade the company to reduce the interest charge made but they are under no obligation to do so.

––––––

Q In a moment of madness, my husband and I sent off £200 as deposit for a time-share but only after reading the literature assuring us that we could change our minds within fourteen days and have our money back. We did change our mind but have had no luck getting our money returned. We've phoned and written to the company concerned to no avail. What more can we do?

A You are entitled to this money and you can report the matter to the Office of Fair Trading, who might be able to prosecute the company, or you might consider going to the police. As long as the transaction was here, it doesn't matter whether the company has a registered office here or whether the time-share was abroad. You should act without delay.

––––––

Q I'd like to put my will in a safe place and wonder whether it is possible to deposit it at the probate office. If so, what is the procedure?

A Yes, you can deposit a will with the Probate Registry for life. The cost is £1 and you can get a free fact sheet from its office. Write to: The Record Keeper's Department, Somerset House, Strand, London WC2R 1LP.

CHAPTER SIX

SHOPPING AND SERVICES

W e might not go so far as to say 'service industries' is an oxymoron but, having suffered ourselves, we do understand the problems which can be caused by people who should make our lives easier. Dressed in a little brief authority, salesmen, supervisors, shopkeepers, suppliers and, dare we say it, even solicitors, can reduce us to quivering wrecks.

Quiver no more! If you're served a bad meal, sold a shoddy item or are still waiting for that furniture you ordered six months ago, help is at hand.

Q My friend and I went for a meal in a rather expensive restaurant. It was a treat to celebrate my friend getting a new job. We were put at a table hidden away in a corner and, frankly, the service was terrible and the food indifferent. We complained but received no apologies. If they didn't want women dining alone, then they shouldn't have accepted us.

What I want to know is whether we would have been within our rights to walk out without paying the bill? We didn't want to cause a scene, but paid and left. To add insult to injury, service was included so we couldn't even show our anger by withholding a tip.

A Why do we so often suffer in silence, seethe and not vent our spleen till later!

If you get a rotten table and awful service and food, don't be afraid *there* and *then* to demand better. If it is not forthcoming, don't put up with it. You can refuse to sit at the table, refuse to accept the food and walk out without paying.

On the other hand, if, ghastly though your meal is, you accept both food and service, you are liable to pay for it in full although it could be worth your while to speak to the management and argue for a discount.

You do have to pay service charges if they are clearly printed on the menu or otherwise brought to your attention before your order. Where service is charged, this must now be included in the cost of the meal and the restaurant which fails to do so commits an offence. Service cannot now be simply tacked on to the bill at the end of the meal. If you are disgruntled with the service, you can dispute its inclusion and if you refuse to pay, you should leave your name and address in the unlikely event that the restaurant can pursue you by legal action for these service charges. Even if you did know of the service charge prior to ordering, you can still complain and argue for a reduction but you are not entitled simply to refuse to pay and walk out. If you do walk out and refuse to pay either for food or service which the restaurant has provided, you may well be committing a criminal offence under the Theft Act 1978, or, in Scotland, under the common law of theft.

———

Q There was a large notice-board in one section of the local supermarket which said 'Caution. Slippery floor.' I walked carefully but skidded across it. Nothing was hurt except my dignity. However, an officious-looking assistant nearby said quite gratuitously, 'It would have been your own fault if you'd broken anything, you know.' Well, do I know that? Would it have been?

A If the assistant had gone to your help instead of being instantly on the defensive, you'd have gone away mollified rather than miffed! Luckily you escaped injury but whether the warning notice would be enough to get the supermarket 'off the hook' rather depends upon the state of the floor. If you were likely to slip, however carefully you walked, then the floor was obviously so unsuitable for walking upon that it ought to have been sectioned off. On the other hand, the supermarket would argue that the notice was enough to ensure that customers taking care would not come to grief.

It all comes down to an assessment of the facts and it is certainly not the case that such a notice automatically provides a complete defence for those seeking to rely upon it. (See also pp. 129, 187.)

———

Q I was on my way out of the supermarket when I was stopped by the manager. He asked to look in my bag which he examined most carefully. Quite a few people I know saw me and it was terribly embarrassing. I hadn't taken anything I hadn't paid for so that was that. But the man barely apologized and I feel very angry. I feel as though my neighbours are looking at me and saying I'm a thief. Do I have any case for redress against the store?

A Apart from a strong letter of protest to the store for the lack of apology there is really nothing else you can do. You were asked and consented to have your bag searched and therefore there is no question of what is called 'false imprisonment'. You were not falsely accused of any theft and so no defamation arises, nor were you prosecuted wrongly, so there was no malicious prosecution. Whilst understanding your embarrassment, the man at the store was just doing his job – perhaps over-zealously and obviously not very politely.

———

Q Please settle a dispute! I say that it is theft for a person to remove an article from a shelf in a shop intending to take it without paying, even if they change their mind and put it back. My friend insists that the stealing only occurs when you leave the shop.

A Your friend is wrong. What you are really faced with, however, is a problem of proof since it is far more difficult to prove that a person intends to steal if they are still within the shop. Nonetheless as a matter of law, if an intention to steal is formed and an article removed with that intent, the act of theft has taken place even if a change of heart follows. (See also pp. 87, 212.)

———

Q Some weeks ago, I was without electricity for twenty-one hours due to a fault in an underground cable. It was a hot spell and everything in my freezer defrosted. The local electricity office agreed that they were responsible for the fault but have refused compensation for my freezer contents, saying that I should have been insured. Can I take this further?

A Whether or not you should have been insured is a matter for you not the electricity company. They are contractually obliged to provide electricity and, as they agree it was their faulty cable which stopped that supply, they are, in our view, also responsible for damage resulting from the supply cut, i.e. your freezer contents. Go back and argue with them.

———

Q We've just moved house and when we unpacked we discovered that the removers had caused damage to some of our furniture. We estimate several hundred pounds' worth of ruined items but the removal firm has said that our goods were moved at our risk.

A Then what were you paying them for? Professional removers ought not to damage goods and, if they do, they should have insurance cover to meet any claim, like the one you can bring in the small claims court for the loss you have suffered.

———

Q My daughter bought an expensive brand name watch at a bargain price from a street trader. The watch stopped working after a week and she then discovered it was not the genuine article. The street trader's attitude is 'tough luck'. Can she do anything?

A In law, the goods are shoddy and she is entitled to her money back, whatever she believed the brand was. More than that is the fact that to sell counterfeit goods is illegal and it could be 'tough luck' for the trader if, as we suggest, your daughter pays a visit to her local trading standards office. (See also pp. 38, 130–37.)

Q I bought a sweater from a well-known chain store and when I went to exchange it because it was too big, I found it was now a sale item. I therefore asked for a refund and protested when this was refused. I was told that I should have gone to customer service if I wanted money back. I argued and eventually was paid the £10.00 difference. Was I right to make a fuss?

A In our opinion you were right! If the store's policy is to provide full refunds on items returned to customer service, then you should have been directed there when you took the garment back so that you could get the full refund and then buy the replacement item at the new sale price on the shop floor. (See also pp. 38, 123, 130–37.)

Q Is a builder bound by his estimate or can he charge more money when the work is completed?

A If the estimate was an offer to do work at a price agreed by you, the builder cannot charge extra. If, however, he was providing only a rough indication of possible costs, then he is entitled to charge more to reflect the true cost of the work. Most people use the word 'estimate' when they really intend to be bound by the price quoted. This is yet another thing which should be sorted out in advance to avoid misunderstandings later. (See also p. 47.)

Q I bought a dress which I knew was too tight but the
saleswoman was very persuasive. I was on a diet and
I told myself I'd lose five pounds and it would look fine.
But I haven't and it doesn't. The nice saleswoman turned
nasty and says I can't have my money back but I can
have a credit note. I don't want one as I need a new dress
and I need the cash to buy it elsewhere. Do I have to take
the note?

A Yes, you do. When you bought the dress, you were well
aware of its shortcomings – or rather your own – and you
are not entitled to reject it unless there is actually a fault with
it. Some shops might even refuse a credit note and would be
within their rights. So your new dress will have to come from
the shop's available stock. Or you could go on a crash diet!
(See also pp. 38, 120, 130–37.)

––––––

Q I saw the perfect outfit for an upcoming wedding. As I
had no money on me, I asked the shop to hold it until
the following day when I would return and pay for it. The
shop agreed but when I went back as arranged, I discovered
that the outfit had been sold in the meantime by an assistant
who did not realize that it was being held. I was most upset
as it was the only one in stock but was the shop within its
rights to do this?

A If the shop had definitely agreed to sell the outfit to
you, then a contract of sale was created and, assuming you
returned to pay for it within the stipulated time, the shop
was actually in breach of that contract by selling it to someone
else. You could have a claim against them for the extra cost

(if any) of having to purchase an alternative garment which might afford you some 'redress'.

Q I was given a credit note for returned goods. When I attempted to make a purchase in the shop for half of the value of the note, the manager informed me that I had to spend the whole lot in one go and could receive no change, nor a further note if I didn't. I protested but eventually bought some goods I didn't really want just to use up the note. Could I have insisted on spending as much or as little as I pleased on the credit note at one time?

A If, when you first exchanged the goods, you were not entitled to a refund but the shop exercised goodwill in taking them back and giving you a credit note, then you take the note subject to any condition imposed by the shop. It may be argued that this is true even if you were entitled to a refund but elected instead to take credit. So it is unlikely that you would be able to 'spend' the note other than as the shop directed. It is always better to get a refund when you are entitled to one rather than taking a credit note which you also take the risk of losing. (See also pp. 38, 121, 130–37.)

Q I bought a freezer from a well-known electrical store. A few days after delivery, the food began to thaw and a good deal of it was ruined. The freezer was obviously faulty and the store replacd it. However, when I claimed for the cost of the ruined food, the store sent me a cheque for the full amount but wrote that they were making payment as 'good-will' and that this was in full and final settlement of any further claims I might have. I am concerned that, in accepting the cheque, I will not be able to claim if my replacement freezer goes wrong.

A Put your worries on ice! If any fault develops in your new freezer, your rights are unaffected by the previous settlement, which related only to your ruined food and not to any claim which might arise for the replacement freezer. By the way, from what you have said, you were entitled to that cheque whether sent with 'goodwill' or not. (See also pp. 38, 122, 130–37.)

Q I've seen a solicitor about a case I wish to bring against my former employers. His advice was totally negative, although I know I have a strong case and former colleagues who are prepared to back me. He stirred himself once to talk vaguely about settling out of court which I don't want to do as the principle is as important to me as the money. Would it be all right to go to another solicitor and, if so, do I have to pay the first man the full fee?

A You are always entitled to change your solicitor, particularly if you feel less than confident with the advice or attention you are getting. However, the first solicitor is entitled to keep hold of the papers entrusted to him by you and all documents relating to your case until he has been paid. So, unless you can manage without them or he is prepared to accept a promise from your new solicitor that the bill will be met, you will have to pay. You can challenge his bill if you believe it to be too high for the amount of work done by asking for what is called a 'taxation', which are independent assessments of what he is entitled to charge. But unless you can show his conduct amounted to incompetence, you will almost certainly have to pay him something.

One word of caution: principles can turn out to be very expensive where litigation is concerned. (See also pp. 104, 109.)

Q Since, in every case brought, there's a lawyer who wins and one who doesn't, how do I find a good lawyer? I've heard some real horror stories!

A Let us say straight away that the lawyer who loses a case may not necessarily be the bad guy, just the one who came second! There are many other people and factors involved when you embark on legal proceedings. Word of mouth is one way of getting a good lawyer. And the Law Society can provide a list of solicitors in your area. You can write to The Law Society, 113 Chancery Lane, London WC2A 1PL or in Scotland, The Law Society of Scotland, 26–28 Drumsheugh Gardens, Edinburgh EH3 7YR. (See also pp. 104, 109.)

Q We arranged for a local upholsterer to repair and recover an antique chair. The work was estimated to take six weeks but many months have gone by and we are being fobbed off with one excuse after the other as to why the chair is not ready. We're now rather worried as the chair is quite valuable and the upholsterer doesn't even answer our calls or letters. What should we do?

A You must deliver an ultimatum in writing to the upholsterer demanding your chair by a specified date. If this brings no result, we suggest that you take advice with a view to legal proceedings. The upholsterer is either recklessly inefficient or a crook and, whichever it is, the time has come to claim against him for the return of the chair or its value, plus damages for the loss of use of the chair.

———

Q I ordered a sofa from a local department store which promised to deliver it on the following Wednesday. They could not give a definite time of delivery but said it would be between 9am and 1pm. I duly took time off work but the sofa did not appear. When I rang the store to complain, they said the delivery men had arrived at 1.05pm to find nobody at home. We then arranged another delivery date. Again I took the morning off work and again there was no sign of the sofa. This time 'the van had broken down' and we arranged yet another date. The sofa was eventually delivered but I lost three mornings' pay as I am a freelance artist. Can I claim any costs from the store?

A We've waited for deliveries which never come but, however infuriating, it is doubtful whether you would have a claim against the store. It seems that you were given the dubious benefit of 'free' delivery when you made your purchase. Such benefit is in the nature of a side arrangement for which no separate payment was made and therefore a claim is unlikely to succeed. You would clearly be in a stronger position if either the delivery time had been an express part of the contract to purchase the sofa, or you had paid the store to deliver the goods.

———

Q My fiancé and I went to a furniture exhibition and ordered a three-piece suite from one of the stands. We paid a deposit and the salesman told us to expect delivery in 6–8 weeks. That was *six months ago*! We have telephoned and chased them up but all we are told is that the furniture is on the way. Frankly, we are fed up waiting and although we really wanted that furniture, we have now seen a suite we like almost as much in a local store. Can we cancel and get our money back?

A We admire your patience in waiting this long! Since you would still like to have this suite, write to the firm and inform them that, as they are well over their promised delivery time, you will now put a time limit on the contract of, say, two weeks, failing which the order will be cancelled and you expect the immediate return of your deposit. It never ceases to amaze us how quickly firms react to such letters and are suddenly able to effect immediate delivery! However, if neither the furniture nor the deposit are forthcoming, you can seek the return of your money by issuing a summons in your local county court, or by applying to the sheriff's court in Scotland.

Q My mother, who is an avid knitter, wanted to buy a knitting pattern in a local shop the other day but the shopkeeper refused to sell her the pattern unless she also bought the wool to go with it. Could my mother have insisted on purchasing the pattern without the wool?

A Afraid not. When anyone goes into a shop, a contract is formed only when the shopkeeper agrees to sell to the customer. The shopkeeper can, therefore, refuse to sell his goods or impose terms for the sale as he wishes. In your mother's case, it seems that the shopkeeper was within his rights but he's probably lost a good customer through lack of goodwill.

Q I am a pensioner and rely heavily on my television for entertainment. Recently, it started playing up and a friend gave me the name of a TV repair man who works from home. He took my television away but within a few days of getting it back, it went wrong again. Since then, I have had to call him out twice. Each time he has taken the TV away to repair it and bills so far have amounted to £150. I realize that I should not have used a potential 'cowboy' operator but can I claim back any of the money I have paid out to him as I am sure he is taking me for an expensive ride?

A You could well have a claim for the return of *all* your money. If you paid for repairs which were plainly not done or have been done badly, then you are entitled to recover the cost of these so-called repairs. The 'small claims' procedure through your local county court would appear to be your best bet to attempt to get your money back.

Q I took an expensive silk shirt to the dry cleaners and when I collected it was horrified to find it had a huge scorch mark where none had been before. It was ruined. When I complained, the manager of the shop casually pointed to a small sign above the counter which stated that all items were cleaned at the customer's risk. Can this be right? Have I any basis to claim?

A No, to your first question. Yes, to your second. Frankly, had the sign been set in stone or emblazoned in neon lights, it would not help the shop one bit. There is an Act of Parliament called the Unfair Contract Terms Act 1977 which was designed to protect customers from shops which attempt to avoid liability with signs like this. Put your complaint in writing to the manager, setting out all the facts and claiming compensation. If that doesn't do the trick, go to your local county court and take out a summons under the 'small claims' jurisdiction. From what you say, you seem to have a valid claim to pursue – go ahead! (See also pp. 118, 187.)

Q We bought a TV set from a branch of high street electrical goods retailers. The remote control went wrong after a short time and the shop agreed to repair it. That was three months ago! We have been in touch with the shop constantly but we are just told that repairs are taking longer than antici-pated. We haven't been able to use the set and we still do not know when to expect the control back. Is there anything we can do?

A It is difficult to understand why the shop did not supply you with a replacement control immediately. At the very least, they should by now have either repaired or replaced yours. You must go in and demand action and furthermore you might be able to claim damages equivalent to the cost of hiring an alternative TV for the period that the set has been out of use. A visit followed by a strong letter ought to get this shop 'switched on' for action to satisfy you.

Q We treated my daughter to lessons at the local driving school for her birthday. We were told to pay the driving instructor for the full course on the first lesson and we gave him a cheque. However, at his request we left the 'payee' blank for him to fill in the 'correct' account name. He gave us an appointment card with the lessons listed on it. After five lessons, I was informed by the school that the instructor had been arrested for theft of driving school funds which he had paid into his own account. The school is now refusing to give my daughter her remaining lessons unless we pay again for them, nor will they refund any monies paid. Can they do this? They say they are not liable for their dishonest employee.

A The driving school is wrong. On their instructions, you paid their employee who had apparent authority to accept payment on the school's behalf. Whether cheque or cash was stolen by him, it was stolen from his employers and not from you. The driving school must bear the consequences of their crooked employee and if they refuse to give your daughter the lessons still due or the balance of your money for these lessons, you can seek reimbursement through the small claims procedure in your local county court.

Q A year ago, we bought our son a violin from reputable suppliers of musical instruments at a cost of nearly £500. From the start, our son had problems in tuning it and six months ago the wood split. The suppliers refused to replace it but carried out repairs and assured us it was as new. However, the violin is still unsatisfactory and it looks as if we are going to have to buy another. Have we any remedy against the suppliers?

A If the violin was, indeed, an inferior instrument then you could well be entitled to recoup at least the difference between what you paid and what it was actually worth. You might even be entitled to the full cost price back if you could show that the quality of the instrument was expressly misrepresented to you. In order to recover anything, you would undoubtedly need an expert's opinion to state the violin was unfit for the purpose for which it was required. (See also pp. 38, 121–24, 130–37.)

———

Q I bought a dress for my baby which shrank after one wash although I had followed the washing instructions. When I returned it to the shop, the manager refused to change it because I had washed it and he could not have it replaced by the manufacturer. It was an expensive dress and had only been worn once. Is there really nothing I can do?

A You can go straight back to the shop and insist on your money back. The goods proved to be deficient and the shopkeeper is legally bound to provide you with a refund regardless of the manufacturer's attitude. Your contract is with the shopkeeper. (See also pp. 38, 121–24, 130–37.)

———

Q My daughter purchased a tracksuit from a stall at our local market. She wore it once but when she washed it, according to the instructions, it shrank and the colours ran. She returned it to the stall holder, who refused to give her the money back. He offered an exchange but she does not want this. Can she insist on her money back?

A Stall holders are in no different a position from shop owners. If the goods are defective then your daughter is entitled to her money back and can (and should) refuse to be fobbed off with an exchange. In view of the man's attitude, we recommend you report the matter to the local market inspector's office and even to the appropriate section of the local authority, both of whom may have some say about his licence to operate the stall. Perhaps if you tell him this is your intention, he'll have a sudden change of heart! (See also pp. 38, 121–24, 130–37.)

———

Q We ordered a glass-topped table. When it arrived, there was just one man to bring it into the house and he was struggling with it. So I gave him a hand because I felt sorry for him, although my wife told me that I shouldn't, in case we dropped it. Is she right that we would not be able to claim compensation from the firm if this had happened?

A If delivery of an unwieldy item is arranged, then responsibility for safe delivery rests with the sellers. If they provide inadequate manpower so that you have to lend an inexpert hand and the item comes to grief, then we take the view that the shop is responsible. However, we also take your wife's point that your assistance could give the shop an argument against you that they otherwise would not have, so although we consider that they ought to bear the costs, you could find yourself landed with a more tricky debate than would be the case if the delivery man alone had damaged the article. You can be *too* helpful!

———

Q We ordered double-glazing from a firm which had completed work on several of the houses in the road. We paid half the money in advance. The men never turned up and, after repeated phone calls, we went to the address on their brochure. We discovered they'd gone out of business. That was the end of our money as we were told eventually. Imagine our surprise and anger when we discovered that the firm is back in business under another name. We've been told that this is perfectly legal and we can't get any money out of them. Is this really so?

A If you paid money over and had an agreement with a firm made up of individuals who have now opened another business, then you can sue the individuals. If, however, as we suspect, they operated a limited company then the only recourse you have is against the limited company, which probably has no money and you are unlikely to receive anything from the liquidator. There might be an element of dishonesty involved with these people and it just might be worth referring the matter to either the Trading Standards Office or the police, or both.

Q We had a wonderful Christmas lunch only to find that the entire family suffered chronic stomach upset on Boxing Day. We suspect the turkey was not as fresh as the butcher had assured us. Do we have any redress?

A As long as you are *sure* it was what you ate and not a surfeit of liquid refreshment or anything else that caused the problem, you are certainly entitled to receive some compensation for the pain, suffering and even, if appropriate, the disappointment of a spoiled Boxing Day. If indeed the bird was the culprit then it is the butcher who is liable to you and your family. Go and talk turkey to him!

Q Imagine my small son's distress when his longed-for clockwork train failed to work after it was assembled. His godparents bought the toy. Can we take it back?

A This is a problem for your son's godparents. Tell them the problem and let them deal with it. The toy can, of course, be returned and either the purchase price refunded or the train replaced with one which works. (See also pp. 38, 121–24, 130–37.)

––––––

Q What can I do about an unwelcome Christmas present? I received an expensive watch which I neither need nor want but I really could do with a new kitchen clock.

A Oh dear, the perennial problem of redundant Christmas gifts! As long as the gift has not been used, the best you can do is take it to the shop where it was purchased, smile and explain your dilemma. Most shops will be prepared to allow an exchange although they are under no legal obligation unless this had been expressly agreed beforehand with the purchaser. (See also pp. 38, 121–24, 130–37.)

––––––

Q Getting ready to 'dress' the Christmas tree, I tested the lights from last year and found they didn't work. I had only used them for a couple of weeks. Is it too late to take them back and change them?

A No! Even though the lights are about a year old, they've had little use and, unless otherwise specified on the box, tree lights are not intended to last only one season. You are certainly within your rights to have at least an exchange, assuming the lights have been used according to instructions and that there is an obvious fault with them. (See also pp. 38, 121–24, 130–37.)

––––––

Q A few days before Christmas last year I organized an 'office lunch' for six of us at a local restaurant. We turned up at the appointed hour only to find the restaurant had 'overbooked' and couldn't accommodate us. Everywhere else was full so we went without our annual treat. How can I avoid this happening again?

A Any restaurant which lets customers down as you have described is in breach of contract and liable to compensate you for ruining your special celebration. Personally, we wouldn't go near that restaurant again but, whichever venue you choose for your next party, let them know you expect your booking to be honoured. Confirm the reservation again a few days before. Incidentally, this works both ways. If you have booked a restaurant table, the onus is on you to turn up or give them fair warning that you are not coming.

———

Q I received a mail order catalogue from which I ordered a dress which never arrived. The company then asked for the return of their catalogue on the basis that I had placed no orders but soon after I was billed for an amount for unspecified goods. I returned the catalogue, never received anything from them but am being harassed by demands for payment. How do I deal with this?

A You must write a letter stating the exact history of events and stressing that although an order was, in fact, placed, the goods were never delivered and you therefore owe nothing. Keep a copy of any letter you write and stick firmly to your guns!

———

Q My husband bought a barbecue kit which he assembled following the instructions. When we first used it, the grill plate collapsed and dislodged a couple of smouldering brickets onto my husband's foot, causing a nasty skin burn and damaging his leather sandal. What are our rights regarding the injury and damage to my husband and the barbecue itself?

A If the barbecue kit was faulty or the instructions either unclear or misleading, then you would have a claim either under the Sale of Goods Act or for negligence. Either way you can claim a refund for the barbecue kit plus damages to cover the injury, ruined sandals and any spoiled food. However, if your husband was at fault in his assembling of the kit, then any claim would most probably be unsuccessful. (See also pp. 38, 121–24, 130–37.)

Q I went to the hairdresser for highlights. When I came out from the dryer, I was horrified. I'm not a punk so green streaks aren't for me! The hairdresser said he could do nothing for a few weeks for fear of damaging my hair but then he'd put it right. Can I claim anything for the time I've spent hiding indoors, afraid to go out for fear of being laughed at?

A You are certainly entitled to claim for distress and anguish. Damages awarded in cases like this are usually related to the particular effect the mistake has had upon the victim. In principle, your claim would be met with sympathy although the damages awarded will rarely compensate fully for the misery you have undergone. Now you know what they mean when some people say that green is unlucky!

Q I bought apples from my local market which looked fine on the outside. Inside they were all bad. Could I have changed them?

A Since you bought them to eat and not look at, you could have changed them or had your money back. The apples were not 'fit for the purpose', i.e. to be consumed. (See also pp. 38, 121–24, 130–37.)

CHAPTER SEVEN

IN THE WORKPLACE

The workplace has become a minefield with laws governing sexism and racism, maternity leave and unfair dismissal. In fact, there's so much going on, it's a wonder any work ever gets done!

We rather enjoy a compliment or flirtatious comment but some men are now terrified to make them for fear of ferocious feminists. Garage mechanics take down their girlie calendars, the office wag wonders whether he dare make a joke about the Welsh and, nerves shattered, daren't light up for fear of the anti-smoking lobby. Of course some conditions and colleagues are intolerable, but let's try to be reasonable about these issues.

———

Q My daughter has been working for a company for two years and last week she was sacked without warning. She was told the company could not afford to keep her. She is shocked and distraught because of the hard work and effort she had put into her job. She was taken on as a self-employed worker and does not know how she stands with regard to her tax or stamp position. Her boss had told her not to worry about this. Can she claim compensation for unfair dismissal?

A If your daughter was self-employed then she cannot claim for unfair dismissal as an employed person can. However, she can claim for a period of notice to which she would be entitled either under any agreement she had made with the company, or, in the absence of such agreement, the law will imply a reasonable period of notice. As a self-employed person her tax and stamp are her own responsibility but she can seek advice from her local tax office to see whether the company classified her properly as self-employed. Depending on her duties, she might be considerd by the Inland Revenue as an employed person for whose tax and stamp the company had a liability to pay. (See also p. 145.)

Q I have worked for many years in a small factory as a solderer. Although fans were installed to extract the solder fumes, these don't work properly and several of us feel very ill at work. Complaints get us nowhere, even when the works doctor was consulted. Can we do anything?

A Your conditions of work could amount to unsafe or unsatisfactory practices and reference to the Health and Safety Executive might be the answer. You should all band together and put your concerns in writing to this body, which may respond by sending an inspector to investigate the problem at your workplace. (See also pp. 140, 148–51.)

Q I was badly injured at the factory where I had worked for fifteen years. I want to claim against my former employers but I have now seen the accident report form which is wrongly dated. It shows that I had my accident six months earlier and the date given is more than three years ago, which means I am out of time to sue. Can they get away with this?

A If you suffered injury requiring treatment, your medical records will support the actual date of your accident. So will the date you stopped work or had time off for your injury. This report alone is unlikely to defeat your claim. A solicitor will know what to look for but you must seek legal advice and start your proceedings without further delay. (See also pp. 139, 141, 148–51.)

———

Q My husband worked in an asbestos factory until 1986. He died two years ago. He was sixty-six and his death was attributed to a stroke. Last week, I bumped into the wife of one of his fellow workers. She told me that her husband had died the previous year of asbestosis. She was bringing a claim against the firm and was waiting to hear the result. She told me I should make quite sure that if I or my children were to develop any illness whose symptoms could be attributed to the fact that my husband worked on the 'blue' asbestos, I should be sure to bring a claim. Her husband had had a very painful illness and death and she felt that people should be compensated, particularly since the workers were not told of the dangers of asbestos. What would be the situation if my children (or I) were to develop symptoms in years to come?

A Many workers were not informed of the dangers of working with asbestos although now there is far greater awareness of the inherent dangers in different kinds of work and controls relating to exposure to toxic substances have been in force in the UK for some years, partly home grown and partly arising from EC directives. However, asbestos has affected and is still affecting not only the people who worked on it but also their families, and even when the symptoms develop years after the last contact with this toxic substance, a claim can be brought. As your husband was said to have died from a stroke, it seems unlikely in your case that his death was attributable to his former working conditions and probably even less likely that either you or your family have been affected. However, should any symptoms develop in the future that could be ascribed to secondary contact with asbestos dust, i.e. where the dust is brought home on the clothes and skin of the worker, then a claim might arise if you could show that the effect upon you was due to unsafe or unsatisfactory practices at your husband's workplace; for example, inadequate facilities provided there for your husband to wash properly and change after his contact with the asbestos. (See also pp. 139, 140, 148–51.)

———

Q Last year I got a job as a manager in a bakery firm. My basic wage was for a ten-hour shift, five nights a week but gradually I was expected to work longer hours with no extra pay. I said nothing as I was anxious to keep the job which I enjoyed. However, one morning I was taken ill just before I left for work and my husband called my employers to let them know I couldn't get in. My boss reacted aggressively and was abusive to my husband before slammning down the phone. The next day, when I complained about my employer's rudeness, I was told bluntly that if I didn't like it I could go. I was upset and did leave but to date my ex-boss has refused to pay my outstanding wages. I would like to recover the money due, which is only £84.00, but I am worried about legal costs involved in any claim.

A You must feel upset by all this. At minimal cost, you can seek a recovery of the sums owed by using the 'small claims' procedure through your local county court. However, you might be entitled to claim unfair dismissal at the Industrial Tribunal or even wrongful dismissal through the courts. The full facts of your case would have to be considered and we strongly urge you to seek competent legal advice, beginning perhaps at your local law centre. (See also p. 159.)

———

Q I work for a large organization and the chance for promotion came up recently. Four of us were shortlisted; the other three were men. The man who got the job is not as good as I am; his qualifications are not as good as mine and I know I'm just as good as he is at staff relations. Is there anything I can do about this?

A The sex discrimination legislation makes it positively unlawful for a woman, otherwise qualified for a post, to be passed over on the grounds of sex. You can attempt to seek justice by applying to the Industrial Tribunal which can rule upon the practices of your employer and award you compensation if your application is successful. Your application must be made within three months and legal aid does not apply, although you may be eligible for advice under a scheme which allows limited services from a solicitor to consider your case, assist with documents and letters and generally guide you. This advice scheme is means tested but is designed to help those who have little money but need someone to point them in the right direction.

However, you must weigh the fact that you might get a reputation as a troublemaker. Unfair? Yes. But it might be worth having a discussion about your future with your present employers to assess their attitude. And keep an eye out for openings with a firm which practises what the Sexual Discrimination Act preaches! (See also p. 154.)

Q My boss asked me to work late and, as I need the money, I was grateful for the offer. Unfortunately, he made a pass at me. I managed to put him off fairly pleasantly but I'm rather nervous. I need the extra cash and he has implied I'll lose my job and not just the overtime if I don't do what he wants. Have I any legal rights?

A You do have rights and if, in spite of your protests, your boss continues his threats, forcing you to leave your job, you might be able to make an application to an Industrial Tribunal on the grounds of unfair dismissal, depending on your length of time in the job and the size of your employer's work force. You must make an application within three months of the termination of your employment. No legal aid is available for such an application, although the advice scheme outlined in our answer to the previous question is worth looking into, or you might seek advice from ACAS. You can also refer to the Equal Opportunities Commission or the National Council for Civil Liberties. (See also p. 146.)

Q I am a twenty-six-year-old man who works for a thirty-five-year-old woman boss. She is forever making passes at me, takes me for drinks after work and tells me that she fancies me, implying that my 'cooperation' might lead to promotion. I don't know how to handle this one. My colleagues already tease me about the boss's attentions and I'd feel like such a wimp if I reported her. Any suggestions? (See below.)

Q I work for a very nice woman boss and was flattered that she took so much time helping me. She takes us all out individually for a drink after work and we all like her. However, last time she entertained me, she propositioned me. I suspected she was a lesbian and that doesn't bother me but I just don't want her to pay me that kind of attention. I'm worried about offending her as I need the job and like it.

A We've put both these questions together as their problem is basically the same. And they prove that the female of the species can be as predatory as the male!

First of all, our advice to both of you is to talk frankly to your bosses. Explain that you are not interested in their sexual advances and hope that this will not affect your career prospects. If your bosses care about their jobs and their employees, they will accept what you say and it should make no difference to your prospects.

However, it is possible that either or both of them might react as a woman scorned. If they do, you can take action. It is accepted that women can harass men sexually and, also, other women just as men can be taken to court for pressing unwelcome attentions on women. You would have to bring your claim to the Industrial Tribunal and show that you have been sexually harassed or discriminated against under the Sex Discrimination Act 1975. Once again we mention the Equal

Opportunities Commission who would, we are sure, be as helpful to men as they are to women in these circumstances.

———

Q I work four afternoons a week. Do I have the same job rights as someone working full-time?

A As a general guide, you have the same rights if you work at least sixteen hours a week. For instance, if you have worked in the same job for sixteen hours a week for two years, your employer cannot fire you without good reason. If you work more than eight hours per week but less than sixteen, the qualifying period is five years. No matter how few hours a week you put in, some legal rights apply to all employees. These include the right not to be discriminated against because of your race or sex, or victimized for trade union activities.

However, it is worth mentioning that if as a part-timer you find yourself first in line to be selected for redundancy, there is a school of thought that this could amount to indirect sexual discrimination as so often part-timers are women. At the present time the UK has resisted pressure from the EU which seeks to abolish all distinctions between full-time and part-time workers. (See also p. 139.)

———

Q My son has recently been sacked from his job with a large company with whom he has been employed for over four years. He believes he was unfairly dismissed and is waiting for the outcome of the company appeal procedure before applying to an Industrial Tribunal. Is this a sensible course of action or is he in danger of any prejudice to his position?

A Any person qualifying for application to the Industrial Tribunal (and this appears to include your son) *must* apply within three months from the date of dismissal. Generally, anything short of being in a certified coma would appear to be insufficient grounds for an extension to this deadline. Your son should put in his application without delay and irrespective of internal procedures. This is a straightforward process and it can be withdrawn if your son's appeal succeeds. (See also p. 143.)

Q My daughter recently left her job as she didn't get on with her boss. She enrolled at an employment agency but has been told that her ex-boss has supplied a reference describing her as lazy and dishonest. She is horrified at these lying allegations. Can he get away with this?

A If your daughter can show that the contents of the reference are lies, motivated by malice, then her ex-boss cannot rely upon his privilege to express opinion about your daughter in this reference because he has been deliberately and knowingly spreading untruths. Your daughter must write a strong letter to him to this effect in order to extract a retraction and apology.

Q I'm very proud of my children who want to earn extra pocket money by working for it. At the same time, I do have some small worries. My son is thirteen and plans to take on a paper round. Is he old enough? Would the employing newsagent have insurance to cover him in the event of an accident or even, heaven forbid, being attacked?

My daughter is fifteen and has been offered a night a week's babysitting. She's very responsible but I feel this is rather young to be in charge of toddlers aged two and four. Once again, I wonder what problems she might encounter if anything went wrong.

A At the age of thirteen your son is old enough to do a paper round as long as the hours of work do not offend local authority byelaws. You should find out from the shopkeeper what is expected of your son and check with your town hall that nobody is falling foul of the law. At the same time you can satisfy yourself that the shopkeeper is properly insured against any mishap in which your son could be involved.

As for your daughter being in charge of little ones – well, this rather depends upon her maturity and good sense, although the parents of the toddlers remain responsible for their children's welfare whilst they are in the care of anyone under the age of sixteen.

We are quite sure, however, that your offspring will cope admirably with their new-found responsibilities, especially with a caring mum like you to keep a close eye on what they are doing.

———

Q I suffer from RSI (Repetitive Stress Injury) and am bringing a case for compensation against my former employers. I earned £10,000 p.a. They have offered me £70,000 to settle out of court. It seems a lot but I'm only forty-two so, hopefully, I've a long time ahead of me! I'm going to need a lot of help as I can do very little in the house or garden and that will cost money. I don't know whether to go ahead with the case, or what to do for the best. I feel I deserve better compensation but suppose I'm awarded less than they have offered?

A First you must take advice from a skilled and experienced personal injury lawyer who would have to look at a number of issues before the amount of compensation can be considered adequate or not. These issues are:

 (i) the merits of your case;
 (ii) whether you have lost all your capacity to work or could do something;
(iii) what your degree of pain and suffering has been and whether you are likely to have any respite from this;
(iv) how your injury has affected other areas of your life, e.g. domestic work, gardening, driving and whether you will now need paid help for these activities;
 (v) how long you would have worked or whether any other health factor may have impinged upon your working life;
(vi) what your injury has cost you so far in loss of earnings or any other expenses.

When these general points and any other factors particularly relevant to your situation have been assessed, then and only then can you and your advisors make a considered decision about the amount of compensation properly due to you. (See also pp. 139–41, 149–51.)

———

Q I've worked for the same company for fifteen years. Three years ago, our typewriters were replaced by word processors. We were told we should have regular breaks from these machines but this, in fact, didn't happen. I've now developed RSI and cannot work, garden, cook, knit or do any of the things I used to do. I'm also in terrible pain.

I've seen a solicitor and am bringing a compensation case against my employers. They deny liability and say I should have taken the rest periods but there was too much work for us to do that. They also point out that I'm the only person in the office to have developed RSI, although last year they brought in an ergonomic expert and replaced all the furniture with 'worker-friendly' stuff. They've now offered me a job, at the same salary, answering the phone but I'm worried that, if I take it, I might have to put up with the pain and get no compensation. And I might have to give up work again later.

A RSI is a fast-growing problem. You might be the only person in your office to have developed it but that doesn't mean you don't merit compensation. One thing is for sure, you certainly cannot accept a telephonist job on the basis that you drop your claim for all your pain and suffering. Equally, if you turn down the new post, you could find it held against you that you had failed to 'mitigate' your loss, i.e. failed to take up a position designed to reduce your losses.

Your lawyers could advice you on the merits of your claim, which seem favourable from what you have told us, but in addition to your actual injuries you could be entitled to claim a sum for your drastically reduced advantage on the open job market even if you now work as a telephonist. (See also pp. 139–41, 148–51.)

———

Q I was so delighted to get a job with a one-man firm which pays very well. My boss could not have been more welcoming or helpful. He put me in charge of the books and, in the beginning, would tell me to enter this or that in a certain way. Now that I am more experienced, I realize that he is fiddling the books. I'm at my wits' end to know what to do. I really need this job but I'm worried that, should the fraud come to light, I would be guilty along with my boss. He doesn't give me any extra money nor would I take it. I think he thinks I don't really know what's going on. What do you think I should do?

A We suspect that you know our answer – resign immediately! When you first started the job, you were ignorant of what was going on. Now, you're in a very different ball game. Not only are you knowingly going along with this man's attempts at fraud but have you realized that, if you are the one keeping the books, he might even be able to say *he* knows nothing about it and you will be wholly to blame?

─────

Q My employers have recently provided me with a chair which has arms. I find this very uncomfortable for typing and I have complained that this design is giving me backache. Can I insist on a different, more suitable chair?

A If poorly designed furniture results in lasting back trouble and you have informed your employers of your problems, then they could be liable to you for injury or loss of income arising from this situation. Point this out firmly at the same time as you indicate your choice of a more appropriate chair for your work. (See also pp. 139–41, 148–51.)

─────

Q My husband was injured at work when the head of a new hammer, supplied by his employers, flew off and struck him heavily on the foot. He went to the foreman who told him that, as the hammer was purchased elsewhere, my husband had to sue the suppliers of the hammer for any compensation. Does he really have to do this?

A No, he does not. Since the Employers' Liability (Defective Equipment) Act 1969, any employee injured by defective equipment in the course of his employment can look directly to his employers for damages. His employers might have a claim against the suppliers but that is their decision and does not affect their liability to your husband. (See also pp. 139–41, 148–51.)

———

Q I have a job which I thoroughly enjoy. By coincidence, I work alongside a man who shares the same date of birth. Now I'm coming up to retirement and he has five years to go. I don't want to leave! Is it legal for me to be compulsorily retired while my colleague isn't?

A Good to hear of a woman who's happy in her work! The European Court has ruled that a woman is legally entitled to work until she reaches sixty-five if she so wishes and this ruling is binding upon all member states of the EU. Therefore, you can retire at sixty or keep at it for another five years if you so wish.

———

Q I am a self-employed, divorced woman and I employ a nanny for my six-year-old son. She is absolutely essential to me and my career. Can I claim a proportion of her earnings against tax?

A No. Although the nanny is employed to enable you to work in the first place, the Inland Revenue will not allow any part of her pay to be offset against your tax as they consider her duties looking after your child to be entirely domestic and therefore separate and unconnected with your actual work. The fact that you could not go to work without employing the nanny cuts no ice with the Revenue – as we have discovered from personal experience. If the nanny also acts partly as your secretary, then you may well be able to claim part of her wages as business expenditure.

––––––

Q I've just been diagnosed HIV positive. My colleagues know that I'm homosexual and it's never been a problem. What worries me now is whether I should tell them. I'd hate it if their attitude to me changed but I wonder whether they have the right to know.

A Legally speaking, being HIV positive (or, indeed, having AIDS) is not a notifiable disease. So this is something you must decide for yourself. Do you have anyone with whom you can discuss it? Would it be an idea to find out from other HIV positive people what they have done in your circumstances? It is entirely possible and understandable that even people who accept your homosexuality might feel nervous about your condition. Obviously, too, the nature of your work might make a difference – if you were a dentist or involved in the preparation of food, for instance.

We feel all these things should be thoroughly discussed with your doctor and other knowledgeable persons before you decide what course to take. The Terence Higgins Trust will be helpful and constructive in this situation and you can contact them at 52–54 Grays Inn Road, London WC1X 8JU; Tel: 0171–831 0330. (See also pp. 167, 210.)

––––––

Q A colleague has asked me to give a reference to his eighteen-year-old daughter who is job-hunting. Although I play squash with him and have a drink, I've only met the girl a few times. If she's like her father, she'll be all right but I wonder: if I give a reference and she turns out not to be what I've promised, can I be held liable in any way?

A Giving a reference usually comes under what is called 'qualified privilege' which protects the writer of the reference. However, it is a somewhat 'grey' area legally speaking and if you provide a glowing report of someone you do not really know then you might find yourself at the wrong end of an action for 'negligent misstatement'.

Frankly, we think you should either decline to provide the reference or ensure that you state honestly the limited knowledge you have of the girl whilst giving appropriate credit to her family background, of which you seem to know more. Tell her dad that a limited reference is all you can properly provide and he can then decide to look elsewhere if he wishes.

———

Q I am a manager in a department store. I had the chance to promote someone recently and the choice fell between two women. They have both been with the firm for the same length of time and their ability is about equal. However, I made my decision on the basis that one woman had a better way with the customers. Now the person who didn't get the job and is black is threatening to sue the firm on the basis that I am a racist and passed her over on grounds of colour. It's not true. Where do I stand?

A Whilst we can have sympathy with the loser in this situation, she can only successfully claim against the firm if she can show that the clear inference can be drawn that her colour was the bar to her promotion. Where, however, she can only point to this one incident where actually the better candidate in your view was promoted, then it seems highly unlikely that she would succeed in any proceedings. We hope your unsuccessful candidate will appreciate this. (See also p. 143.)

———

Q I applied for the job of receptionist with a large firm. I was called for an interview and when I was ushered into the manager's office, I knew at once I wouldn't get the job. He looked quite shocked when he saw me. I am black but my name is Scottish and, in fact, the first thing he said was 'Oh, I was expecting someone quite different!' I didn't get the job and I know it was because of my colour. Is there anything I can do about this?

A Yes, you appear to have been the victim of discrimination. You should report the matter to the Commission for Racial Equality who can, if they feel it is merited, investigate this firm's policy on recruitment. If they find that there appears to be a policy of discrimination being operated, they will take up your case and the firm can be prosecuted. It doesn't get you the job but it may make the firm revise its thinking about staff and cease to be 'shocked' when unexpectedly interviewing a person of a different hue. (See also p. 143.)

———

Q I have been working as a contracted freelance beauty writer for a newspaper which involved attending many functions and receptions to learn about different products. Because of cutbacks, my contract was not renewed. I rang a cosmetics company to find out why I had not received my invitation to their annual reception and was told that one had been sent to me at the office and a member of staff had replied to say that she would be attending in my place. As the invitation was addressed to me, I'm very angry that the letter (and, presumably, others) was not sent on. Is there anything I can do about it?

A Probably not. Had the letter been marked 'Personal', this would have constituted an invitation personally to you. But in this case, what the firm wanted, we imagine, was a representative of the newspaper, someone still on the staff. The best advice we can give you is to inform all your contacts to deal with you directly at home in the future and hope the invitations still come in.

———

Q I'm three months pregnant and my boss has insisted that my holiday entitlement must be used to take time off work for antenatal checks. Is he entitled to do this?

A Absolutely not! In the normal run of pregnancy, you are entitled to have paid time off for antenatal care and your holiday time should be left intact. The Department of Employment (whose address is in the phone book) will supply you with full details of your rights as a working mother-to-be, including your entitlement to maternity leave and pay. (See also p. 156.)

———

Q I have got the most adorable baby daughter. I took maternity leave (on full pay) to have her, fully intending to go back to my job. Now I just don't want to but I'm worried. I know they won't have any problems replacing me, but will I have to pay back the money I've had?

A Congratulations! Nice to know you're nappy-happy! You certainly do not have to repay any monies to which you

155

would have been entitled as Statutory Maternity Pay, as you would have received that whether or not you later decided to return to work.

However, if you have received more than the Statutory Maternity Pay by arrangement with your employer, then whether or not you have to repay the extra amount depends upon the exact terms upon which this was paid to you. If you were paid upon condition of your return to work, then your employer may demand repayment of the extra amount from you. (See also p. 155.)

————

Q I've been working part-time for a company for nearly three years now. I was married six months ago and we are talking of starting a family. If we do, I'd like to go back to my job and I'm wondering what my position is regarding length of leave and pay. I work a twenty-hour week.

A Every working woman is now entitled to maternity leave and time off to attend parentcraft sessions and antenatal classes. This entitlement applies regardless of how long you have been in your job or how many hours you have worked.

Furthermore, for all women taking maternity leave, your employer cannot count this leave as a period of absence from work for any purpose, for example, pension rights or holiday entitlement, and you are entitled to be treated as if you had never been away so as to take advantage of pay rises and rights not to be unfairly dismissed.

If you are not offered your own job or an equivalent alternative on your return to work, you can take your employer to the Industrial Tribunal, to which he will have to justify his actions.

You are also protected from having to work nights and your

employer cannot put any restrictions upon the length of time you choose to breastfeed your new child.

If a woman has been employed for any time up to two years then she is entitled to fourteen weeks maternity leave but this time off does not have to be paid.

In your case, however, you clearly qualify for both maternity leave and pay since your employment exceeds two years with the same employer and more than sixteen hours per week. You can claim your maternity leave and the right to return to your job as long as you inform your employer that you intend to exercise this right. At least twenty-one days before you leave work, you should give notice that you are taking maternity leave and you intend to return. If, in fact, you change your mind about going back to work, you can inform your employer after the birth and likewise you must give notice to your employer at least three weeks before you intend to resume your job.

In view of the length and hours of your employment you can take a legal maximum of forty weeks leave, that is, eleven weeks before the birth and up to twenty-nine weeks after, although both you and your employer can postpone your return for up to a further four weeks if you have medical grounds and your employer, for his part, gives proper reasons.

Whilst you are on maternity leave, you will be entitled to Statutory Maternity Pay if you have paid National Insurance contributions which allows you up to ninety per cent of your earnings for six weeks followed by twelve weeks at a lower rate. This lower rate is set by the Government and can change and this is also payable for a period of up to eighteen weeks for women who have worked for at least six months up to and including the fifteenth week before the baby is due.

Whatever the length of time in your job you should always

check the position with your employer (or union representative) and your own contract of employment as you might find your company provides even better arrangements for leave and pay than those described above which are, of course, set down as a minimum entitlement under the law. (See also p. 155.)

———

Q I'm a heavy smoker and now the firm I work for has announced that they are banning smoking from the office. We've taken it to mean that if we don't obey the ruling, we will be fired or have to resign. Are they within their rights in doing this?

A It seems they are. A man who brought a claim against his employers recently, stating that a smoking ban amounted to constructive dismissal, had his case dismissed by an Industrial Tribunal. This ruling conflicted with a 1984 Industrial Tribunal decision but since the medical evidence that passive smoking – i.e. breathing in other people's smoke – can be a health hazard, it is felt that similar bans are justified on medical grounds.

Before the ban is introduced, your employers should talk to the staff and perhaps arrange a smoking area where nicotine addicts can light up in their breaks.

However, we would point out that resigning or being fired are not the only choices. You could give up smoking. Think of the money you'd save and how well you would feel!

———

Q My daughter had a Saturday job in a local shop but was sacked without pay at the end of the day when the owner accused her of making unauthorized phone calls. She denies this and is owed a whole day's pay. Was the owner entitled to act as he did?

A Even if your daughter had been using the phone, her boss was not lawfully entitled to withhold her wages. We would advise that she make a claim for her lost money, if necessary through the small claims procedure in the county court. If she tells the shopkeeper what she intends to do, he might well stump up the money on the spot. We hope so. (See also p. 142.)

———

Q Some two years ago, my colleague and I were asked to take on the extra payroll work which was caused by the sudden departure of the wages clerk at our firm. Our then boss promised us a lump sum payment of £500 each for the work but he has since left and our new boss refuses to honour the promise. He claims that the firm has no obligation to meet this payment as the extra work was simply part of our job descriptions. Is he right?

A He may be right legally even if morally his conduct is hardly admirable. If, in fact, the wages clerk's work was really part and parcel of your job (which seems unlikely) then the promise of extra money to perform what you are paid to do anyway had no legal force. If, however, you actually did do more work than you were obliged to do, then you can and should press for payment. (See also p. 142.)

———

Q I'm terrified. I'm always cracking jokes and have a bit of a reputation as the office wit. I'm never malicious but now an Indian colleague (with whom I've always got on, or so I thought) says he might report me for a flippant remark

I made about his sun tan. Honestly, I'm not racially preju-
diced. I like the guy.

A Are you sure he's not having a joke at your expense? We
do hope so. It's a sad fact that some people now see the
prospect of financial compensation for 'hurt feelings' in
the lightest of remarks. We think your case is an instance of
something that should be laughed out of court.

However, in the light of recent decisions at the Industrial
Tribunal, a person who is the butt of racial or religious jokes
may not feel like laughing and neither will the joker when
he/she is faced with a large bill for damages.

The best advice to give you is to make sure your victim
knows that any flippant comment made by you is entirely
non-malicious; even better advice in this day and age – avoid
racially sensitive comments altogether. (See also pp. 75, 210.)

CHAPTER EIGHT

MEDICAL MATTERS

W e sometimes think it would be easier to set one's own broken leg than get information from a medical practitioner. And it's when you're not feeling well that you're least able to assert yourself. But patients don't have to suffer in silence. We do have the right to ask questions, gain access to our medical records and, if we're not satisfied with the treatment we receive, to do something about it.

———

Q Last year I suffered a miscarriage during the early months of pregnancy which caused me great distress. I now believe that this occurred because I was prescribed certain drugs by a locum doctor who was running my GP's practice whilst she was on holiday. I feel that I should be able to claim for all that I have gone through but my GP refuses to release my medical records, claiming that they are 'privileged'. Is there anything I can do?

A Yes. Medical records are not 'privileged' – contrary to
the popular belief – and if you are embarking on possible
litigation you can obtain an order through the courts compel-
ling your doctor to produce your records. In any case, however,
the Access to Health Records Act 1990 allows you to apply
in writing to your doctor for your health records where these
consist of any information about you, including opinions of
either your GP, or any other health professional who reported
to your GP. The drawback of this Act is that it restricts
access to records made after 1 November 1991, although there
is allowance in the Act to provide earlier records if these are
needed to make sense of the more recent compilations. (See
also pp. 163–64, 169–72.)

———

Q I have just changed my doctor because I was not very
satisfied with her. I've just managed (with the help of my
husband) to get off the tranquillizers she prescribed for me.
I feel my previous doctor might have implied in my medical
records that I'm a nervous, slightly nutty, sort of person (I
promise you I'm not) and I'd like to see what she wrote about
me. Can I insist on seeing my previous records? I don't want
to get off on the wrong footing with my new GP.

A The medical records can now be sought under the 1990
Act as we have described in the answer to the previous
question. We would advise, however, that it may be more
helpful to you to have a frank discussion with your new GP
about yourself and your concerns as to what may have been
written about you rather than embarking upon what could be
seen as confrontational tactics at this early stage of your
relationship with the doctor. GPs, we imagine, will take a bit
of getting used to having to show records on demand and if

you can achieve a satisfactory result without the demand, this could be of benefit to you in the longer term. (See also pp. 161–64, 169–72.)

———

Q I recently applied for life insurance and have been turned down. I wonder whether this has anything to do with the medical report from my doctor which the company asked for? I am in good health but I do have a stressful job and have seen my doctor occasionally when I have had difficulty sleeping. Is there some way I can find out why I was turned down and what was contained in this report?

A Yes. Under the Access to Medical Reports Act of 1988, your doctor must show you a copy of his report unless he feels in his professional judgment that it would not be in your interest to see part or all of it. This must be done within six months.

If, for any reason, you had wanted to know what the doctor was going to write *before* the insurance company saw it, you should have contacted him within twenty-one days. Any insurance proposal form will include details for making these arrangements with your doctor.

We do feel that, for your own peace of mind and whether the doctor is willing to show you the report or not, you should go along to see him. After all, he might just tell you that it's not a good idea to smoke 100 cigarettes a day! (See also pp. 161–64, 169–72.)

———

Q My cousin suffers from a very painful bone disease which required hospitalization. The local hospital where she had all the preliminary tests and X-rays said they didn't have a bed for her. She ended up in a (very good) hospital but it was a thirty-mile round trip from her home, which made visiting very difficult (and expensive) for the family as she was there for a year. Surely if you pay taxes and N.I. stamps, you have a contract that you should receive treatment at the nearest hospital?

A Not every hospital is equipped to cope with every complaint and when you require treatment of any specialist nature, the best you can hope for and expect is that you will be referred to the appropriate hospital with proper facilities to provide you with the treatment you need. This may mean travelling further afield but we are sure you would find a longer journey preferable to being referred to a hospital which has less qualified staff or unsuitable equipment for your ailments, however inconvenient it may be for you and your visitors.

If, however, the lack of a bed was the only problem with the original hospital, any ensuing delay with her treatment, giving rise to a deterioration in her condition, would put the NHS at risk of a claim. (See also pp. 161–64, 169–72.)

———

Q I was attending a dentist for root canal work when my work took me to another part of the country. I went to a second dentist and he continued the treatment. As I was still in pain, a friend recommended yet another dentist who treated me privately and said the root treatment was now finished.

The pain, however, started up again and I went to the casualty department of the local hospital, where they treated me for neuralgia. The pain continued so I went to yet another dentist. He X-rayed me and said that, in his opinion, my jaw had been drilled during the root canal treatment. He treated me and the pain has, at last, subsided.

However, the third dentist I saw has just presented his bill plus interest. I told him I would not pay as the treatment was not satisfactory. He has started using a debt collector. I have written to him to say that I intend counter-suing for damages and the cost involved in finally getting my tooth treated. What are the steps I should take to complain about the dentist and do you think I have a case for compensation?

A Any complaint regarding dental treatment which might amount to misconduct or over-charging or possibly negligence can be referred to the General Dental Council at 37 Wimpole Street, London W1M 8DQ; Tel: 0171–486 2171. However, in order to sue a dentist for compensation you need to establish from an independent dental expert that your treatment was actually negligent and in your case you would have to show that the dentist at whom your legal guns are aimed was in fact the one who caused your problems. Given the rather involved history of your dental experience, we would advise you to seek an initial view from a solicitor who specializes in medical negligence cases. (See also p. 173.)

Q What sort of comeback does a person have in the case of wrong diagnosis? I had a smear test recently and was told everything was all right. But you do read of cases where women are diagnosed as 'negative' and then they develop cancer.

A The theoretical answer is that any wrong diagnosis might be the result of a negligent act on the part of the person making it and a claim can be made to cover the consequences of such a diagnosis as it can be with any medical negligence.

In practical terms, however, it is not easy to sue the medical profession successfully since it is so difficult to establish that they have acted unreasonably or negligently. In cases of suspected medical negligence, you should contact a most helpful organization called Action for Victims of Medical Accidents (AVMA) at Bank Chambers, 1 London Road, Forest Hill, London SE23 3TP; Tel: 0181–291 2793. (See also p. 173.)

———

Q I am twenty-one and obsessed by a fourteen-year-old girl. She isn't a typical fourteen-year-old. We don't look 'wrong' when we're out together. I plan to marry her when she is of age. She is very keen that we have a sexual relationship and I must admit I'm finding it very hard to resist. Would it be possible for her to get the Pill from her doctor?

A Yes, it is entirely possible for the young lady to obtain the Pill from her GP and possibly desirable if *she* is thinking of indulging in a sexual relationship. However, it is also the case that if you do have sexual intercourse before your 'girl' reaches her sixteenth birthday, you would be committing a criminal offence since you know she is under age, however mature she looks or how 'right' you are together.

We would strongly advise that you both contain yourself for at least two years, when she will have more judgment and you will know whether your 'obsession' is a passing infatuation or the real thing. (See also p. 170.)

———

Q Four years ago, my dentist announced he was taking early retirement to see something of the world. I was sorry because he was an excellent dentist. Last week, I discovered that, in fact, he died last year of AIDS. He had, obviously, been diagnosed as HIV positive when he gave up his practice (which was private). I'm very sad as I liked him very much. However, I wonder what the legal situation would be if I were to discover that I am HIV positive (this would certainly be as a result of going to my former dentist). Would I have any claim to compensation?

A If you were indeed to find that you were HIV positive and you could show that the source of this finding was this dentist, then you would be entitled to claim compensation from his estate for your anxiety, stress, illness and any loss suffered by you by reason of this diagnosis. However, your claim would only succeed if you could show that the dentist was negligent in passing the infection on to you. We trust, however, that this dentist's legacy to you will remain pleasant memories and not long-term problems. (See also p. 152.)

Q I am a nineteen-year-old student and I'm two months' pregnant. I cannot possibly have the child. I've two more years of studies ahead of me and then I want to work before settling down. Also, although it might sound despicable, I realize I am not very keen on the father. I told him I was going to have an abortion. To my horror, he went completely wild, said he loved me deeply and wanted me to be the mother of his child. He says that he will take me to court to stop me terminating my pregnancy. Can he really do this? I'm going to have the operation anyway, but I'm worried in case he can take proceedings against me afterwards as he keeps going on about it being his child as well as mine. I'm desperately worried as I don't want either the college authorities or my parents to find out and he says he's going to make a 'stink' about it. I wish I'd never told him now but just gone ahead and done it.

A However deeply he feels, the father of your unborn child cannot stop the termination of your pregnancy, nor has he any grounds for 'proceedings' either before or after an abortion. If he carries out the threat to make public your predicament then there is little you can do to stop him and you will have to explain (if necessary) the situation as best you can and live with it. We're sure your parents and the college will show tolerance and sympathy. In the end, we feel a woman must decide the best course for herself but must do it in a responsible way. It isn't very responsible to sleep with, let alone get pregnant by, a man you're 'not very keen on'. (See also p. 3.)

Q My boyfriend and I have lived together for over a year now. I became pregnant and, as I did not want a child, I had an abortion. If this should happen again, I would have another abortion. My boyfriend is strongly opposed to this and feels that he should have some say in the matter as the father of the unborn child. Does he have any legal rights to stop me having an abortion?

A No, he would have no rights whatsoever in any decision that you made in respect of a pregnancy. Maybe the day will come when the wishes of the 'father' will be taken into account in such circumstances – but we're not there yet. It does seem, though, that you and your boyfriend have a lot of talking to do about what kind of future you want together. (See also p. 3.)

Q I am sixteen and earn a very low wage. I have been told that I need extensive dental work done but I am very worried about the cost and wonder whether I am entitled to have the treatment carried out on the National Health. I simply cannot afford to pay for it and neither can my parents.

$\mathbb{A}$ As you are under eighteen, you are entitled to attend for your necessary dental treatment and receive it free of charge, irrespective of your income. However, we should emphasize to everyone that whether you are dealing with a dentist, builder or hairdresser, you should establish in advance what the cost will be.

––––––

$\mathbb{Q}$ I had an operation two years ago to improve my nose. It was done privately and I discussed it fully with the surgeon in advance. When I was visited the following day, it was by a completely different man who said he was my surgeon's partner and had done the operation. I'm not very happy with the result of the operation and I'm furious that it wasn't performed by the man I discussed it with. Can medical people do this and do I have any comeback?

$\mathbb{A}$ How very distressing for you. Whether the man was better or not than his partner, you have the right to the person you consulted and, more importantly, contracted with. Generally, private operations are governed by an agreement between the patient and the particular surgeon and if the surgeon fails to carry out the operation, he is liable to you if something has gone wrong or if you have paid for services which you never received. As with any claim which involves injury to the person, you have three years in which to bring your case from the date that the injury occurred – in this case, your operation. (See also pp. 161–64, 170–72.)

––––––

Q Cervical smears and breast screening tests are recommended but they're not easy to get. I had a smear test two years ago and everything was supposed to be all right, but now I'm not sure and I'd like to go back for another. Do I have a right to insist upon another test now even though I am not strictly due for one for at least another year?

A If you have genuine concerns and wish these to be investigated, then any responsible doctor could be expected to act upon these and provide a suitable test for you. If a doctor unreasonably fails to respond to your fears and you become ill as a consequence, then you would be entitled to make a claim against a doctor and he could be liable to you for any pain and suffering you have – whatever small comfort that might be! (See also pp. 161–64, 169–72.)

Q I cannot talk to my daughter about anything at the moment. She's fifteen and mixes with a crowd we know very little about. She doesn't appear to have a regular boyfriend but I think she is on the Pill. Do the parents of underage girls have the right to know if this is the case? Personally, I disapprove of the Pill strongly, not on moral but on medical grounds.

A Your point was debated right up to the House of Lords who finally decided that parents do not have the right to know if their doctor has prescribed the Pill for under-age daughters.

As you find you can't talk to your daughter, why not try writing to her as you have done to us? You could put down all your fears for her health and safety and show her how much you care. (See also p. 166.)

———

Q I'm one of those people who are too nervous to contradict a doctor. Now I've found a lump in my breast and I'm extremely worried. I'm determined to assert my rights (if any) and say that I don't want a mastectomy until all possible forms of alternative treatment have been discussed. But I'm told that I'll have to sign a form before the biopsy agreeing to the removal of the breast if the biopsy is positive. What are my rights?

A You should never be nervous about speaking your mind or voicing your concerns to anyone, including members of the medical profession. You do have the right to insist upon only the biopsy being performed without the removal of the breast should the biopsy prove positive. However, the surgeon can refuse to carry out the biopsy if he considers it inappropriate to be bound by only a limited consent. If he does refuse, you can ask either him or your own GP to refer you to another specialist who might be more sympathetic and willing to act upon your wishes. Before entering hospital, it's best to find out what the surgeon's reaction will be to your views. (See also pp. 161–64, 169–72.)

———

Q I have been referred to hospital for a gynaecological problem. My own doctor is a woman and very sympathetic; she makes me feel relaxed and unembarrassed. But she says she doesn't know whether I'll see a man or a woman at the hospital. Do I have the right to insist on seeing a woman doctor?

A You have the right to make a request but, sorry, that's as far as it goes. We do understand your feelings. It's rotten feeling below par and then facing up to something or someone who adds embarrassment to your condition. All we can say to you is: please, put your health first and see the doctor as a doctor, not as male or female. Most doctors or hospital authorities will do their best to act upon any request you make but it just isn't possible to stipulate in these circumstances unless, of course, you can afford to go privately. (See also pp. 161–64, 169–71.)

Q I had a vasectomy three years ago and started an affair a year ago. I told my lover that there was no problem with contraception as I had had the operation. Now she tells me that she is pregnant and threatens to tell my wife. I don't know which way to turn. My wife will probably want a divorce and I don't. I don't want any more children (we have three), which is why I had the 'snip' in the first place. Can I sue the surgeon?

A We would have thought suing the surgeon was the least of your problems. First of all, are you sure that the baby your girlfriend is expecting is yours? Could it be a 'false alarm'? Has her doctor confirmed the pregnancy? Put it to her that you have had this operation and make quite certain that there is no possibility of the child being anyone else's before you go ahead and sue.

In general terms, if a vasectomy or any other sterilization proves ineffective and its failure was due to negligence during the medical procedure, you can sue and obtain damages to reflect either distress and the cost of the termination or the stress and some costs of having the responsibility of a child.

However, there's more water to go under the bridge before anyone leaps to the divorce or maintenance courts. At least try to counter your lover's threats by checking with your doctor whether your vasectomy is still effective. And till then – take care! (See also pp. 165, 166.)

————

Q My husband and I have seen painful deaths in our families and are agreed that we do not want to go through the same thing should we become terminally ill. Would you please tell us how the law stands on euthanasia? We have decided to 'help' each other to die, should it become necessary. However, neither of us wants the surviving partner to run the risk of murder or manslaughter charges. Surely a person has the right to decide his or her own fate?

A Well, yes and no is the answer! Nobody can stop you committing suicide if that's what you want, but everything changes the moment another person is involved. Imagine the outcry and demands for investigation if very sick patients in homes and hospitals were to die suddenly. Your own question raises the debate of euthanasia, namely who ultimately does decide whether life should end or not? By definition, if it is not by your hand (which used to be but is no longer a criminal offence), then someone else has to administer the lethal dose, withdraw drugs, turn off the machine, etc., and a fine line exists between 'killing' and 'letting die'.

At the present time, any form of euthanasia, i.e. an active step to end the life of another, is an unlawful act punishable with criminal prosecution. Indeed, except in the clearest cases, doctors have to seek court guidance to turn off machines which are keeping alive those in irrecoverable coma, particularly where there could be a challenge to that decision.

173

Ultimately, this is an area of the law which raises more moral than legal questions and it remains to be seen whether eventually we go down the American road of the concept of the 'living will', which some US states have introduced with a view to helping terminally ill patients decide their own fate.

CHAPTER NINE

ON THE ROAD

W hoever coined the phrase 'transport of delight' has obviously never travelled on the London tube in the rush hour! Yet running your own car is no easy ride either: problems with parking, other drivers, accidents and insurance claims are all calculated to drive us mad. Even pedestrians can walk into difficulties.

Travel anywhere can bring problems. Your luggage doesn't turn up, holiday arrangements are changed and where do you stand? Let's face these questions head on.

——

Q I was stationary at traffic lights when I was hit in the rear by a van whose driver told me that his brakes had failed. My car was badly damaged and I injured my neck. However, I have now found out through my insurers that the van driver was not insured. Is there any way that I can be compensated for my injury or my losses – in particular my no-claims bonus, as this affects my premiums? The driver owned the van.

A Any loss you suffer can be recovered from the driver himself – if he is worth suing. If not, don't waste your time and money. However, there is a body called the Motor Insurers' Bureau which does cover claims for loss and injury where the party at fault is uninsured or disappears, and you should seek professional advice as to how to go about instituting such a claim. (See also pp. 180, 190.)

Q My car was run into from behind and I took the registration of the car and the name and address of the driver. My car was severely damaged and I was injured and shaken up. I've now discovered that I was given false details by the other driver and I'm frantic about how to go about getting compensation.

A The DVLC at Swansea should provide details of the keeper of the car from the registration number and you can then try to find out who was driving. If all else fails and you can find neither the keeper nor driver of this vehicle, the Motor Insurers' Bureau should compensate you both for your injuries and the damage to your car. (See also pp. 180, 190.)

Q I was running for a bus and I'm sure the driver saw me but he drove off. I tried to jump on but slipped and hit my knee against the railing, which put me out of action for a month. Can I sue the bus company?

A Unfortunately, if you leap for a moving bus, on your head be it – or, in this case, on your knee! The fact that the bus driver may have seen you might make him inconsiderate but it still doesn't make either him or the bus company legally liable for your efforts to crack the urban 100–metre dash. (See also pp. 178, 182.)

———

Q My elderly mother suffered a nasty knee injury when she was literally thrown from her seat on a bus which had braked sharply and suddenly. The bus driver claimed to have stopped to avoid a dog which ran into the road and the bus company has denied responsibility for my mother's injuries, which still give her a lot of pain. In view of what they say, is it worth pursuing a claim?

A It could be worthwhile pressing your mother's claim. If the bus driver was even slightly negligent, the bus company would have to meet the claim in full. However, if it seems the bus driver acted entirely reasonably, then your mother's claim would be unsuccessful. (See also pp. 178, 182.)

———

Q I was sitting on the bus when the child behind me spilled her soft drink over me. The back of my jacket was soaking and I had to have it cleaned. The child's mother apologized profusely but got off the bus very quickly before I could mention compensation. What is the situation here? Apart from a few hours walking around in a stained jacket, I then had a cleaning bill to pay.

A We are so sympathetic. It's high time that eating and drinking on public transport, apart from trains, were banned. Some people can't go three stops without stuffing their faces. Talk about the chew-chew train! Anyway, to answer your question: a parent is not responsible for a child's activities unless it can be said that the child's conduct ought to

177

have been under close supervision and regulated by the parent. This clearly depends upon the age of the child and what he's doing! Unfortunately for you, we do not believe eating and drinking come into this category from a legal point of view. The practical solution is to avoid children who are guzzling on public transport. You might also try complaining to the bus authority who, after all, must have some responsibility for what happens on their vehicles. Smoking is now banned; why not eating and drinking? (See also p. 81.)

Q I had an accident on a bus last year in which I suffered an injury to my arm and shoulder. I'm still having physiotherapy and I am also experiencing panic attacks on buses. Despite repeated letters and calls to the bus company, I've had no response to the claim form I filled out. What should I do now?

A This is an instance where you need the clout of professional help. Find a local solicitor who deals with accident claims – many solicitors advertise their services in the local papers or directories. He/she will advise you on the merits and worth of your claim and help in pursuing it. You may be entitled to legal aid to help you in this matter. (See also pp. 177, 182.)

Q Just one week before our honeymoon, we were informed by the tour operator that the special hotel suite we had booked was no longer available. We were offered either our money back or a double room in the same hotel. With the wedding so near, we accepted the room but it took the edge off what should have been a very special time. Could we also claim compensation?

A If the tour operator is a member of ABTA (Association of British Travel Agents), you should be able to claim reasonable compensation for your disappointment. Even if the tour operator did its best to offer alternative accommodation or your money back, the late notification of the material alteration to your confirmed booking could make the operator liable to you under the ABTA Code. (See also p. 193.)

———

Q My car was severely damaged when my husband, who was driving it, skidded on oil and drove into a wall. My insurers have so far refused to pay me out on the basis that I did not name my husband as a likely driver when I filled out the proposal form and that he had had a drink/driving conviction and a twelve-months' ban about three years ago. I did pay a premium for comprehensive and 'any driver' insurance so I cannot understand how they can be entitled to adopt the attitude they do. Can you advise me?

A Most insurance companies ask the question and expect an answer as to who, apart from the insured, is likely to drive the car. A husband or wife is often an obvious candidate and if they or anyone else is named, the insurance company expects to be told about their driving record since it might affect the amount of the premium and even whether cover will be granted at all. Your insurers are clearly suspicious that you did not name your husband on the proposal form precisely because of his drink/driving conviction. Ultimately, the facts regarding this omission will be the deciding factor as to whether you can persuade your insurers (or a court) that they ought to pay up for the damages under the terms of your policy. (See also p. 97.)

———

Q Last year I was involved in a serious car accident as a result of which I suffered multiple injuries. I was in a coma for two weeks and after I was discharged from hospital, I discovered that the police were taking no action against the other driver as there were no independent witnesses. I have now recovered from my injuries but I wondered whether there was any authority from whom I could claim compensation?

A The fact that there were no independent witnesses does not mean that you cannot bring a claim of negligence against the other driver. It all depends on the facts of the case as to whether you would recover compensation and, of course, it would be your word against that of the other driver. However, you could pursue your claim in the court and if you could show that there was some fault on the part of the other driver then you could at least recover damages for some of your injuries. If there is merit in your claim, you could qualify for legal aid to bring your case and if the identity of the other driver is unknown (or he is uninsured) then you could recover damages from the Motor Insurers' Bureau (M.I.B.). Your solicitor will advise you. (See also pp. 176, 190.)

———

Q As I approached a pedestrian crossing, I proceeded as I saw no one waiting to cross. I was almost at the crossing when a young woman rushed in front of my car. Although I braked, I was unable to avoid hitting her although, fortunately, she was not seriously hurt. Despite her insistence to the police that it was her fault, I have received a summons to attend the magistrates' court. I am distressed beyond words as I have always been so careful on the road.

A Why, oh why, do some pedestrians think that a crossing gives them a divine right to walk (or run) in front of a moving vehicle? They forget that they do not possess divine immunity from injury if they are hit!

Although you don't say so, we expect that you have been summonsed for failing to accord precedence at a pedestrian crossing. Strictly speaking, this is precisely what you did, since a pedestrian – even a kamikaze one – has an absolute right of precedence on a crossing. Nonetheless, although you were technically at fault, we would hope that the magistrate exercises sensible discretion and gives you the discharge you deserve.

Incidentally, in any civil suit by such a pedestrian claiming damages for her injuries against you, the issue of fault would be considered and if the fault was found to be substantially or totally that of the pedestrian, as appears the case here, then it is likely she would get little or even nothing by way of compensation.

———

Q I got up from my seat on the bus as it was approaching my stop. It lurched suddenly and I was flung to the ground. I got up and told the conductor I was going to make a complaint. He said that the rules are that you should only get up when the bus has stopped. I took his number and the bus's number but because of what he said, did nothing about it. My friend was with me at the time. Now, two years later, my knee still hurts and the doctor says I've developed arthritis which might have been caused by a fall in the past. Is there anything I can do? Quite frankly, if I'd waited for the bus to stop before getting off, it would have started up again before I'd reached the exit. And, anyway, suppose I had been a standing passenger?

A If indeed you had been a standing passenger and fallen when the bus lurched to avoid a car in its path, you would have no comeback unless you could show negligence on the part of the bus driver. There lies the problem. To succeed in any such claim, you need to show the bus driver was at fault and since you have to prove your claim, it would not be enough merely to show the bus jerked and you fell.

The fact that you got up to get off before the bus stopped would not in itself be a bar to a claim in negligence (if negligence can be proved).

After this passage of time, your chance of success is remote but since you have three years to bring a claim it might be worth writing to the bus company. But don't hold out too much hope. (See also pp. 177, 178.)

———

Q I've just been fined for speeding – I was about four miles over the limit. Fair enough. But I've just read of a case in the next town where a culprit who exceeded the limit by twenty miles an hour has been fined less than I. Not fair! Why aren't transgressions like this treated equally with everyone being fined the same for a first offence and then more – but still equally – for any further offence?

A In the system of British justice you can be absolutely certain of the sentence in respect of murder, which carries life, at one end of the spectrum and, at the other end, fixed penalties, e.g. for parking on a yellow line. In between there are theoretically as many variations as there are courts and although judges and magistrates are given guidelines and tariffs, it is sometimes the luck of the draw. True, it can seem unfair but if a sentence seems wildly out, you can appeal to a higher court.

———

Q Reading about people dressing up as policemen and attacking lonely women on motorways and elsewhere, I feel very nervous. If I am stopped in my car and I don't think it's by genuine policemen and drive off, what happens if they *are* genuine? Can I be taken to court for obstructing the police in the course of their duty? It is very worrying.

A Yes, it is. This also applies to men who come to the door claiming to be gas or electricity meter readers. In these cases, if you're not expecting them, you can close the door and ring the appropriate office to see whether they are genuine and we would advise this as it's better to spend a little time on being cautious. However, back to the motorway. Every police officer should carry a warrant card and you can and should insist on seeing it to satisfy yourself that the person in question is a police officer. Whilst an impersonator might get hold of a uniform, you can feel fairly certain that the holder of a warrant card is the real McCoy and entitled to your cooperation. If you do drive off in the face of a genuine request from the police to stop, you could find yourself falling foul of the law. On the other hand, if you have a real doubt as to the identity of the persons who stop you, you may be wise to drive off – but play safe by reporting to a police station at the first opportunity.

———

Q I parked on a meter outside a friend's house and when I went out to feed it, a traffic warden warned me to move my car. The street was virtually empty and I told her that it was ridiculous but she insisted. Isn't this crazy?

A Yes. But the traffic warden wasn't crazy, merely implementing a rather silly (to our mind) law but one which would seem fairer if the street hadn't been empty. Feeding meters is against the law; even driving off and coming back to the same meter within a specified time limit is illegal.

———

Q It seems that cyclists have taken over the pavements in London. It's obviously illegal for them to be using them but what can one do about it? One cyclist almost knocked me down the other day, didn't apologize and whizzed off before I could do anything. As they don't have number plates so one can report them, is there anything a humble pedestrian can do?

A Reminds us of the old joke: keep death off the road, drive on the pavement! Seriously, though, the only practical solution is to report the matter to the police in the hope that they will keep a look-out and catch up with these selfish and dangerous pavement hogs! It is indeed unlawful to cycle or drive on the footway and this has been the law since 1835! We think this law should be enforced more vigorously since serious injury can be caused with little chance of compensation for the victim.

———

Q A police car was obviously on a 'chase' and, unfortunately, when the 'villain' shot over the red lights, the police car followed but spun out of control and landed on the bonnet of my car. On hearing the sirens, I had stopped in the junction. I wasn't hurt but my car was badly damaged and I am informed that, as the police were on duty dealing with an emergency, I will have no claim. Is this true that I can recover none of my loss from the police?

A No, it is not true! All of the emergency services are under the same obligation to drive with due care and attention on the road as we ordinary mortals. Obviously, greater leeway is given to those services to bypass traffic restrictions and signs, but only if it is safe to do so. If it is manifestly unsafe or their driving and control creates a traffic emergency or accident, then they are as liable as we are.

Q My car was badly damaged when it was struck by a fire engine which had jumped the lights on its way, apparently, to answer an emergency call. I have been told that I will not recover the cost of repairs to my car as the fire engine had the right of way at the traffic lights even though the lights were showing green in my favour. Is this correct?

A Any vehicle answering an emergency does not automatically have a right of way at controlled junctions, including traffic lights. They do not have to comply with traffic signs or signals, but only if they take reasonable care to see that it is safe to proceed. You may well have a claim if you can show that the firemen failed to take reasonable care when they crossed the lights and hit your car.

Q I often see people driving around with very young children in the front seat of the car. It's dangerous, I know, and often tell the driver concerned (sometimes the air gets blue!), but is it illegal?

A There is a very good law in Spain which states that children under the age of twelve should not ride in front unless special provision is made for them. Since 1988, in this country, any child can sit in the front passenger seat as long as he or she is properly restrained. This can mean an ordinary seat belt where the size of the child makes this appropriate but, of course, a very small child cannot be secured except with a special harness and such a child should not be allowed in the front.

———

Q I got on the bus and found to my horror that I had only a £20 note and a ten pence piece. The bus conductor was very unhelpful and said it was the rule that only exact change was accepted. The lady next to me lent me the fare but it set me wondering – could he have turned me off the bus?

A If the bus was clearly one of those which demands exact fare payments only and you knew this, or ought to have known from clear signs before you got on board, then the conductor was entitled to refuse your proffered note and ask you to leave the vehicle. Otherwise, what you offered was legal tender and the conductor could not reasonably refuse it, nor would he be entitled to turn you off.

———

Q Going through an automatic car wash in the local garage, I heard a loud 'clunk' and when I emerged, I found a great dent on the roof of the car. I complained immediately but the garage manager pointed out a 'disclaimer' notice (which I hadn't seen), just above the push start button. Can the garage really rely on this notice to avoid paying for the damage?

A Any disclaimer notice must be clearly displayed or pointed out before you pay for or (in legal terms) contract to have your car washed. Clearly, this was not the situation here and

186

we consider it unlikely that this notice will help the garage if they try to resist your claim. (See also pp. 118, 129.)

Q I bought a second-hand car through the evening paper and paid cash for it. I tested it myself and it seemed fine. The owner told me that he had had no trouble with it so I went ahead with the purchase. I've only had the car for a month and I've been told by my garage that the engine needs to be replaced at great cost. Can I return the car and get my money back?

A Possibly, if you are able to prove that when you bought the car, the condition of the engine was such that even the most ignorant of car owners *must* have known the the car would require major surgery and his assertion that he had had no trouble must then have been false. In practice, it is not always easy to prove and generally you are far less protected in any private sale than if, for example, you had bought from a dealer. This is why people are advised to use experts from the motoring organizations to check over cars before they go ahead and buy them in private deals.

Q My car broke down some miles from home. I pushed it off the main road but, after locking it, I had to then leave it as I had an important appointment. I was unable to organize a garage to collect the vehicle for some ten days but when I returned with the mechanic to the spot where I had left the car, we discovered it had been completely vandalized. My insurance company is now reluctant to meet my claim, saying that I was negligent in abandoning the car and not dealing with it sooner. Can they really refuse to pay me out?

A Generally, insurance covers negligence – whether your own or others'. Your insurers would have to show that your conduct was so irresponsible as to amount to a reckless disregard for your vehicle before they could refuse to pay you out. Since you had to leave the car but returned to deal with it at the earliest opportunity available, it seems that you could insist on a settlement. However, you should seek legal advice to check your policy which is all important in deciding whether or not you acted in clear breach of any of its terms. (See also pp. 90, 99, 101.)

———

Q I recently bought a car through an advert in the local paper, only to find that the car had been stolen and was sold to me with false number plates and false registration documents. The seller has now disappeared. Do I have any rights to resist the original insurers of the car who are now claiming that they own the car and are seeking its repossession?

A Unfortunately for you and your hard-earned, now sadly departed cash, you acquired no right of ownership (title) when you purchased the car since the 'seller' had no such rights to pass on to you. The insurers, no doubt, paid out when the car was stolen and they, therefore, became the legal owners and are entitled to possession of the car. You, regretfully, became the innocent victim whose rights and money disappeared into the night with the rogue who sold you a financial disaster. You should, however, contact the police as this man might well be inserting other advertisements for property which isn't his to sell. (See also pp. 90, 99, 101.)

———

Q My common-law husband was killed in a car accident last year when a lorry ran into the side of him. The lorry driver was at fault since he came out of a side turning without looking. I had been living with my common-law husband for four years and we had one child who is now three years old. As we were not legally married, am I able to make any claim for myself or our child?

A Although not legally the widow, you are entitled to claim for yourself as if you were the widow because you had been living together for more than two years prior to the death of your cohabitant. Your claim will be on the basis of your dependency on his income and the size of the claim will depend upon his earnings, prospects and age.

Your child is entitled to be treated in exactly the same way as a legitimate offspring in any compensation claim. In Scotland, you would have the rights of a widow by obtaining a court order confirming that you were 'married' by 'habit and repute'.

———

Q My dog is normally well-behaved and I occasionally let him walk freely along our street. The other day, however, he saw a cat, ran into the road and caused a car to swerve violently. It missed my dog but hit a lamp post. Fortunately, no one was hurt but am I liable for the slight damage to the car?

A Both pets and young children should be firmly held at all times! As your dog was unrestrained then, yes, you could well be held responsible for the damage caused whilst the dog was under, or in this case, out of your control. If you have no separate insurance for your pet, check your household insurance policy as this ought to cover you for an event like this. (See also pp. 23, 27, 29, 58, 207–8.)

———

Q My husband was involved in a minor car accident last month. He was blameless and the other driver accepted responsibility but then turned out to be uninsured. If we claim on our own insurance, we will lose our 'no claims' bonus which will cost us more than the repairs. Is there any help for innocent motorists caught out like this?

A There could well be help from the Motor Insurers' Bureau. As you had your own valid insurance and your car damage was caused by an identified although uninsured driver, you seem to satisfy the requirements for the M.I.B. to consider your claim. Contact the Bureau at Milton Keynes and find out whether you are eligible for compensation. (See also pp. 176, 180.)

———

Q We had just come to a stop on a parking deck of the cross-Channel ferry when there was a thump at the back. It turned out that the car behind had run into us. The driver blamed the man directing the traffic for waving him on and refused to accept any responsibility for the shunt. Our car was damaged but from whom do we claim the cost of repairs?

A It is incumbent upon a driver to look where he is going, whether under direction or not. Therefore, whether he likes it or not, this driver should be liable to you. If he feels that the ferry company bears some responsibility because of the actions of their employee, that is a matter for him and them, not you. (See also pp. 176, 180.)

———

Q This summer we went on a 'two-resort' holiday which required a flight transfer from one to another. On arrival at the second resort, we were one suitcase short. Our tour representative was very helpful and within a couple of days the case was located and delivered to our hotel but not before we had had to buy swimwear and sun-tan oil which had all been in the missing case. Can we claim the cost of these items even though they did turn up fairly quickly?

A You can claim the reasonable cost of anything bought whilst awaiting the return of your own property so long as you needed the items in order to enjoy your holiday. Since you wanted to swim and sunbathe in those days without your suitcase, we would think it entirely reasonable for you to have bought swimwear and sun protection and be reimbursed for their cost. (See also p. 192.)

Q We were due to fly to Italy for a holiday when our flight was abandoned just before take-off when the plane ran into a grass verge and we were all badly jolted. A new flight was eventually organized but it required a lengthy journey to another airport in an old, draughty, bumpy coach. Due to this coach journey I suffered a stiff neck which ruined our holiday and caused me months of pain. I made a claim but it has been rejected as being too late on the basis that the time limit for suing airlines is only two years. Is this so and is there anything I can do?

A The time limit is, indeed, two years if your complaint arises from an incident on the plane itself. As your problems stemmed from the coach journey, you have three years in which to claim. Make it clear to the airline that the coach journey caused your injuries. But act quickly! (See also p. 90.)

Q My husband and I have just returned from our holiday abroad which was ruined for us by the non-arrival of our luggage until two days before we were due to come home. Although we managed to buy some clothing and toiletries, we were basically without decent holiday clothes for the entire fortnight. The tension of waiting each day on the offchance that our suitcase would arrive, and the frustration of barely managing with what we had, spoiled the entire trip. We have been offered a paltry sum by way of compensation from the tour operators but I think we should have all our money back. Are we entitled to this?

A We really feel for you and wish we could tell you that you can recover the entire cost of your disappointing holiday. Regrettably, you are only entitled to the costs of the essential items purchased whilst waiting for your luggage to arrive plus a reasonable amount to compensate for your distress and inconvenience. This amount would not, we fear, meet anything like the cost of your holiday but hopefully it would go a little way to make up for such a rotten experience. (See also p. 191.)

Q I booked a winter holiday in Tenerife but, just a few days before I was due to go, my travel agent phoned and said we had to take a different flight from a different airport. This meant that a much more expensive train journey was involved. Can I charge the travel agent for the extra expense involved?

A Generally speaking, the travel agent acts on your behalf when he books your holiday and cannot be held accountable to you for any extras you might be called upon to pay. You need to investigate the precise circumstances for the change in itinerary and also check the conditions of booking (the inevitable small print). If by 'travel agent' you really mean the tour operator then you could well have a valid claim for the additional expense, as this was incurred by a failure to provide exactly what was originally agreed. You should look again at the brochure and travel details of your holiday booking to see whether you have a cause and a case for complaint. (See also p. 179.)

———

Q We were driving in the country when I ran over a rabbit. We stopped, saw we could do nothing as it was dead and my wife suggested we took it home to eat. We did. I was telling a colleague about this accident (and the rather tasty supper which ensued) when he said to me that I had broken the law, that you are not allowed to keep any game you knock down although anyone coming along afterwards may do so. Is this correct?

A Yes, it is! This is a law which probably dates back to William the Conqueror's day. The idea behind it is probably to stop us going out and killing everything in sight. If, however, you come across an animal or bird which is already dead, it is permissible to take advantage of someone else's carelessness or accident.

It's amusing to think of modern man (and woman) driving forth in our Minis and Mercedes in order to trap the night's dinner! We don't think you'll get into any trouble about your rabbit stew but the strict letter of the law is to let not just sleeping dogs but dead pheasants, lie!

CHAPTER TEN

ANY OTHER BUSINESS

I f you haven't found the answer to your problem so far, we hope, at last, you'll find it here.

———

Q For the second time, I have been called to do jury service. I am self-employed and was involved in a big job when I got the first call. I explained and was excused. I don't have a specific reason not to be a juror this time, just that times are hard and I want to keep myself available in case anything turns up. It would be a problem for me if I missed a job and it worries me that a case might drag on. Could you tell me if one is properly compensated for one's attendance? I would like to do my duty as I believe in the jury system.

A And so do we! The jury system is not perfect, of course, but the concept of 'twelve good men (or women) and true', considering a case objectively and without personal involvement is something we can be proud of.

Assuming you do your jury service, you will be paid an allowance, although this is hardly going to equate with a salary for a good job. If you are called for what is likely to be a very long case, you can be excused if this could interfere with work or work prospects. You can ensure that your jury 'stint' is limited to one or more cases of short duration and we are sure that both you and the jury system will mutually benefit from your giving up a couple of weeks of your time.

Q Is it still the law that a wife cannot give evidence against her husband? And what is the position if the wife is her husband's assistant? I ask because I've got to have some tricky dental work and my dentist's wife is also his nurse. If anything were to go wrong, could she be called upon to give evidence? And, of course, vice versa.

A In answer to your first question – no! In fact a husband or wife is able to give evidence against the other in all types of proceedings whether civil or criminal unless, in the case of criminal proceedings, they are jointly charged. However, whether a spouse can be compelled to give evidence against the other is another matter. In criminal cases where the witness is the victim of violence at the hands of his or her spouse or where the spouse is charged with certain types of offences of violence or sex involving a victim under the age of sixteen years, then a husband or wife can be forced to give evidence against the other. In civil cases, on the other hand, no witness can be forced to give evidence that will incriminate his or her spouse.

Q I have been pestered for the last couple of weeks by obscene phone calls. The caller obviously knows quite a lot about me and, although I've never done anything really outrageous, I wouldn't like people to know about certain things in my past which is what this man threatens. I called the police but they say they can do nothing about such phone calls and can only act if there is a physical assault. They were very sympathetic and suggested I might change my phone number but I don't want to do this as it would involve me in a lot of bother and maybe a loss of work as I work from home. Is it really true that the police can do nothing in such cases?

A It is a criminal offence under the Telecommunications Act 1984 to use the telephone system to send offensive and obscene messages. Unfortunately, the police have to know who to arrest even if you were actually being threatened with physical harm, which would constitute an assault. The police could act if you had any suspicion of who the culprit was. Likewise, if you knew the identity of the caller, you could bring a civil action against him which would result in an injunction to stop this legal 'nuisance'.

As it is, the only solutions would be to a) get a piercing whistle and use it every time you get such a call; b) do nothing and hope the caller gets tired of his stupid antics; c) change your number, but if it's a business phone you can hardly go ex-directory and so you gain little from this option, or d) best of all, contact British Telecom, who are most helpful with a service to monitor and intervene on your calls which we think is the most satisfactory course in your case. (See also p. 198.)

———

Q I finished with my boyfriend six months ago and, since then, he's harassed me constantly. I get phone calls at all hours, often in the middle of the night. Or the phone rings in my office and the receiver is replaced when my colleagues or I answer it. I know it's him. And I've been receiving junk mail by the ton and I know he's behind it. I had a word with the police and they were very sympathetic but say there's nothing they can do unless I am physically harassed. Do you have any suggestions?

A The police, rightly, will not intervene unless the criminal law is broken and, as they have told you, unless you are physically harassed. However, the civil law will come to your rescue albeit on a carthorse rather than a charger. You can apply for an injunction against your ex-boyfriend to stop this harassment which carries the threat of imprisonment for contempt of court if he does not obey the court order. The procedure, although effective, is somewhat cumbersome and you will probably need legal expert assistance to set it up. Remember, too, that you must be absolutely certain and be able to persuade a court that it is your 'ex' who is causing all this trouble. (See also p. 197.)

Q My elderly mother was attacked in the street. Her handbag was snatched and she was knocked to the ground. She was shocked and bruised, her nose was broken and her lip badly cut. Her attacker has not been caught but, even so, is there any chance of her receiving some compensation for this attack from the police or some Government body?

A Yes, there is a body from which your poor mother can claim well-deserved compensation. It is called the Criminal Injuries Compensation Board and if you write to them at 19 Alfred Place, London WC1E 7LE or in Scotland to Blythswood House, 200 West Regent Street, Glasgow G2

4SW, they will send you details of how to apply for compensation. If you and your mother have any problems with the leaflets or forms, we are sure your local citizens' advice bureau or law centre will be glad to help. They will advise whether your mother's injuries qualify for an award, as a minimum for compensation exists.

———

Q Ten years ago, I was convicted of a shop-lifting offence – an isolated incident – for which I was fined £40. I have since remarried and I have not even told my husband about my conviction as I was so ashamed at what had happened. I am now very worried as my husband wants me to go to America with him and I understand that the visa application form requires information to be given regarding any convictions. As this offence was so long ago, do I still have to declare it on the form, or can I consider that the slate is now wiped clean?

A Under British law, your long-ago conviction is regarded as 'spent'; in other words, you are generally entitled to treat this unhappy episode as if it had never happened. However, when dealing with visa applications for a foreign land, you may well be expected to disclose the fact of this conviction to satisfy their legal requirements. We would recommend that you write to the American Embassy for guidance on this point. They will not deal with any enquiries by phone.

———

Q There have been a lot of attacks on women and three rapes in my area over the last six months. When I was on holiday in France, I bought a cylinder of gas which I plan to use if any man attacks me. However, my friend says they are illegal (I bought it quite openly in France) and that, if I used it, I could be prosecuted. Surely if I used it in self-defence, it would not be an offence? How is a woman supposed to protect herself?

A Good question! Karate, judo, handbags and umbrellas appear to be the expected tools of trade in self-defence for women. Gas cylinders are definitely not on the list, any more than knives, guns or knuckle dusters. Anything that is designated as a weapon is generally considered offensive and is illegal to carry in Britain, even if intended for defensive purposes only.

Perhaps less devastating and more feeble in their effect than a gas cylinder, a perfume spray or pepper pot aimed at an attacker might be some use and a whistle is always handy!

Q How far can you go to defend yourself against an assault? I've taken to carrying a small knife with me as I live in a dodgy area but a friend says I could be charged if I wounded someone, even in self-defence.

A If you are attacked in your home or in the street, you are entitled to use any reasonable force to ward off the attack. This can include the use of a weapon to hand, such as a kitchen knife or heavy object. You cannot actually carry a knife or other weapon with you in a public place as this is an illegal act even if, perversely, its use might be legitimate self-defence in certain circumstances. The use of reasonable force is also permitted if you intervene on behalf of someone you see being attacked.

Q I was raped four months ago. I got home, closed the door and did nothing about it. I was so shocked and I just couldn't face anyone – not the doctor, the police, my family. Now I've come to terms with it. I read a case in the local paper about another victim and I'm sure it's the same man. I can't help feeling guilty because if I'd reported it, this man would have been stopped. Is it too late for me to report it now? If I do, will I have to go to court?

A First of all, don't blame yourself for a perfectly natural reaction. Few people feel like going through an ordeal twice by having to report the crime as well as suffering it. But, as you point out, only by reporting crimes can the perpetrators be stopped and you will find the police very sympathetic.

It is *never* too late to report any crime, although it is right to say that the earlier a crime is reported, the greater chance the police have of catching a criminal and securing a conviction. As for going to court, it is generally necessary and expected that the victim of a crime gives evidence about it, particularly in the area of physical assault, including rape. If, however, there is evidence apart from your testimony that would seem sufficient to secure a conviction, then you might just be able to avoid having to relive this episode by giving evidence in court.

———

Q Having completed my shopping in the local supermarket, I was leaving my car parking space when I was confronted by a runaway trolley which damaged my car. I immediately saw the manager who said he was unable to do anything. However, if I now make a claim on my insurance I risk losing my no-claims bonus. Can I hold the supermarket responsible?

A Oh, those demon trolleys! We sympathize but you would only have a claim against the supermarket if you could show that the damage to your car was caused by fault on the part of the supermarket or its staff: for example, if the trolley area was on a slope which allowed unsecured trolleys to run, unchecked, across the car park; or if a member of the staff had pushed the trolley into the path of your car. Without this kind of evidence, you would find it hard to succeed in a claim against the supermarket who would *not* be liable for the negligence of its customers.

———

Q I was sitting next to a man at dinner last week who told me he has dual nationality and two passports. His father is American and his mother English. It started me thinking about the whole question of dual nationality. I had always thought that in cases like this, the person had to decide which nationality to take when he/she reached the age of majority. It seems a bit unfair that someone should be able to pick and choose what they want to be at any given moment. I suppose that, if Britain were to introduce conscription, this man would quickly claim he was American, and vice versa.

A Let's hope we never need have conscription again – and we wonder whether he pays two lots of taxes!

To answer your question, it is entirely a matter for individual countries to stipulate whether their citizens can acquire nationality of another country and hold both dual citizenships, or whether an individual must choose which country he/she belongs to and at what point that choice is to be made.

———

Q A friend recently asked me to carry a kidney donor card. I was happy to do this but was surprised that he didn't seem to realize that you are not technically dead when an organ is removed for transplant, only brain dead. I wonder how many people realize this? It doesn't alter my decision but it might affect others'. I also started thinking about the whole situation: is it *legal* to remove organs from a live person?

A Well, yes – with consent, it is indeed legal to remove kidneys in order to donate one to another in need. However, it is not permitted to remove any organ without the consent of the patient *or* for gain (i.e. where the patient is to receive payment), or, obviously, where death would result!

Q I recently placed a block advert in our local paper and paid for it in advance. When the advert was published, there were several mistakes and the paper offered another advert at reduced cost or a partial refund. I opted for the refund but the paper is now insisting that all I can have is a line advert at the back of the paper. Can they do this?

A You were entitled to have a full reprint of your advert (minus errors) at no extra cost but since you were actually offered a refund and accepted this, you can now insist upon the paper honouring this offer to you.

Q I was a member of an amateur writers' circle. The leader of the group was a very nice man who had had short stories published in various magazines and was working on his second novel. He'd had one published some years previously although it hadn't been a particular success. One of the exercises he gave the class was to invent titles for different genres. I came up with a rather good thriller title. Now I see that his second novel is to be published and it has my title. I'm furious as I wanted to use it myself some time and, even if I hadn't, he didn't ask my permission. Is there anything I can do?

A Maybe he'll send you a free copy! Frustrating and annoying though it is, there is no copyright in titles. In any event, you positively volunteered this title for general consumption when you evidently could not resist displaying your talent in this class exercise. What a pity for you that you didn't get your book written first. We're sure that you will think up an even better title in time – but keep it to yourself!

One thing you could do, though, is inform fellow members of your circle of what he has done. And if the circle is organized by a local education authority, tell them. He deserves it!

———

Q As pensioners, my friends and I have often attended our local town hall which organizes tea dances. When I last went, I was crossing the dance floor when I slipped and fell and broke my wrist. A lot of people had noticed the floor was unusually slippery and complained about it that afternoon, describing it as an 'ice-rink'. The council has refused to pay me any compensation, saying a dance floor has to be highly polished and it was up to me to take care. Is there any point in pursuing a claim?

A Yes, there is. Whilst the floors do have to be suitably polished for dancing, a line is drawn where a floor is so slippery as to create an obvious danger – or where perhaps patches of polish may have been inadequately buffed so that hazard areas are created. If you have supporting witnesses as to the unusually slippery condition of the floor then you could well show that on that afternoon the council had negligently created a danger for those people, including yourself, who might be expected to be using the floor that day. (See also pp. 48, 52.)

————

Q I had an affair with a pop star who gave a series of concerts in our town last year. I was very thrilled about it and wrote letters with all the details to my friend who had gone to work in London. Now she tells me that she has been offered a large sum of money by a newspaper to talk about the singer and she intends using extracts from my letters. Can she do this?

A You know what they say: Do right and fear no man; don't write and fear no woman!

Seriously, you let yourself in for this one. Generally speaking, as long as information is true there is no bar on its publication, but in this instance the information was intended for your so-called friend's consumption and to that extent was confidential. Any use by her of the information in the letters could be seen as a breach of confidentiality and the court may well agree to put a stop to the publishing of any material extracted from your letters or information gained from you. Furthermore, any attempt by your 'friend' to quote directly from your letters could certainly be stopped since the copyright in the letters belongs to you and the publication of the whole or any part would be actionable as a breach of copyright and you could certainly prevent this by way of a court injunction. Next time you feel the urge to put pen to paper – write a diary and lock it away!

————

Q I joined a postal book club and after ordering and paying for the required number of books, I exercised my rights and wrote to the club cancelling my membership. Since then I have regularly received a book every month and despite further letters and phone calls, they keep coming. The books are still wrapped, unread and unwanted, and I am now getting demands for payment. Help!

A Help is at hand! Your choice of action is as follows: either calmly write and inform the club that the books were neither ordered nor wanted and await collection by them *or*: simply pop them back into the post with 'return to sender' written on the package and without postage. You are not obliged to go to any expense or trouble. If the books remain in your possession for thirty days after the club has been notified as we suggest, or six months if you don't trouble even to write, then you can treat the books as a gift to you and the book club is not entitled to any payment whatsoever.

———

Q I was telephoned by a newspaper reporter recently for my comments on a neighbour who is involved in a criminal case. He was very easy to talk to and I'm afraid I rambled on a bit. As I was a bit worried about what I might have said, I rang him and he repeated some of the things I was supposed to have said. I asked him not to use a few of them as, on reflection, I didn't mean what I'd said. He became quite officious and said that not only was he going to use them but he had recorded our entire conversation. I really have two questions. Can a journalist quote what you've said (and I'm sure I said what he says I did) even though you've changed your mind? And, since he didn't tell me he was taping our conversation, is it legal to use it?

A If you volunteer information to a journalist – knowing he is a journalist – then you must expect to see your words in print! Discretion is always the better part of frankness where the press is concerned and so, yes, the journalist can use the information he has been given. As to whether a conversation can be recorded when one party knows nothing of the recording device, generally, apart from the laws relating to media broadcasting, anything that can be heard by ones ear can quite legally be recorded electronically and thus the journalist is entitled to publish what he recorded since you were aware of his status when you spoke to him.

———

Q My children's pet rabbit was savaged by a dog which ran into the garden whilst it was out walking with its owner in the nearby park. Our pet had to be put down and I am most upset, particularly as the owner merely called off his dog and walked away. Can I do anything even though I know it won't bring our rabbit back?

———

A This insensitive dog owner could be liable to you for the value of your pet and even, perhaps, your family's distress. The owner of an animal is liable for injury or damage caused by his pet if either the characteristics of the pet or its responses to certain circumstances are likely to bring about such damage or injury. The fact that the dog was unrestrained and permitted to trespass on your property adds weight to your claim. You, or the police on your behalf, might also succeed in obtaining a control order on the dog by a summons in the magistrates court or an interdict in the sheriff's court in Scotland. (See also pp. 23, 27, 29, 58, 190.)

———

Q My dog, who is very boisterous, jumped up at a friend to greet him and accidentally tore the lapel off his jacket. My friend insists I replace the jacket but it wasn't new although it did come from an expensive shop. I'll replace it for the sake of our friendship but would like to know that I'm not legally obliged to do so. Is that right?

A Although your friend has to buy a replacement jacket at today's prices, he does seem prepared to make a profit out of your good nature.

You could argue that you have no legal obligation to replace the jacket if your friend was aware that your dog is prone to effusive greetings. More likely, you would be liable but only to the extent of the value of the jacket just before it was torn.

You might well count your blessings that your dog did not knock your friend off his feet and cause more serious damage – to his person. Remember, people who own dogs must exercise control over them, or risk unleashing ill feelings in others! (See also pp. 23, 27, 29, 58, 190.)

———

Q Please settle an argument. I say that religious instruction classes in school are compulsory. My friend says it's a matter of parental choice. Who is right?

A Religion, sadly, can cause many arguments! However, in general parents have the right to have their children excluded from either religious assembly or instruction. In those schools which have a religious foundation, parents normally find that separate arrangements can be made for their children to opt out of religious activity altogether. In any state school, the parents are entitled to arrange for children to receive alternative religious instruction either in the school itself or outside, in school hours, as long as this does not interfere with their general schooling or with the school's programme. The Government seems to have changed its mind a number of times about the requirements in schools to teach religious studies. If you need to resolve the issue at any time you can contact the Department of Education for their latest decision.

————

Q I'm a twenty-six-year-old married woman and mother of two. A year ago, I had an affair with a man I'd met at the tennis club. It petered out but I had a telephone call from him last month and he told me that he is HIV positive and his partner (a man – he also confessed to me that he is bisexual) is suffering from AIDS. I told my husband about the affair that night as I love him very much and I knew it wasn't fair to put him at risk (if I've not already done so). He was horrified, moved into the spare room and tells me he wants a divorce.

I will, of course, be going to my doctor and am praying that I don't have the virus but, if I do, do I have any comeback against this man who has literally ruined my life?

A What a tragic outcome from a casual episode. Morally, this man has a lot to answer for but legally you have no more comeback on him than if you had caught flu, unless he knew he carried the virus at the time of your affair and failed to disclose this to you; in that case, you could argue a case against him although it is far from certain that the results of such a claim would be resolved in your favour. In any event, how can you be adequately compensated for your ruined married life?

Unhappily, the result of your affair is far reaching and teaches us all that the days of 'free love' may well be over as the consequences may far outweigh the fleeting pleasures.

We hope by now your tests have proved negative and you can try to start afresh. (See also p. 152.)

Q I am Japanese and over here in England for a three-year spell. I'm a keen golfer and would very much like to join the local club. It is a long-established club and has turned down my application, saying they have a long waiting list. I have been told this is not so and that other foreigners have also been denied admission. Is there anything I can do about this?

A Well, we rather feel, to paraphrase Groucho Marx, 'Would you like to be a member of a club that would have you as a member only because they were forced to?' If the answer is 'yes', you are likely to be disappointed. The Race Relations Act permits certain associations, such as private clubs, to restrict its membership to defined racial groups as long as there is no specific reference to colour in its restricting rules. There could be, for instance, Japanese golf clubs here which do not accept non-Japanese members.

It's a difficult situation as we do think people have the right to socialize with whomever they wish while at the same time we sympathize with those who want to 'join in the party'. Why not find a club which welcomes allcomers? (See also pp. 75, 160.)

Q I've invented a kitchen gadget. I think it could be a real winner. Could you tell me how I go about protecting my invention?

A Inventing something can sometimes be easier than protecting the legal rights to it. You need to take out a patent for it. Get in touch with the Patent Office [Department of Trade], 25 Southampton Buildings, London WC2A 1AY.

Q I saw a man being mugged in a fairly busy street. I think I could recognize his attackers but I made myself scarce because I was afraid of being hurt and I just hoped someone else would help. I feel very guilty. If I went to the police, could I ask for complete confidentiality or would I have to give evidence if the attackers were caught and brought to court? Also, can a case be brought against someone like me who doesn't do anything to help?

A To deal with your second point first: there is no legal offence committed by someone who 'turns the other way', even if you have suffered moral guilt. Frankly, it is very difficult in this day and age to 'have a go' since most people rightly fear for themselves and some brave souls have come off badly when they have sought to intervene in an attack. Don't feel guilty – even the police don't encourage public 'help' in violent situations.

As to remaining anonymous, if you now report the matter you could ask for confidentiality but then you would be of little assistance in bringing the attackers to justice since the police really need the identification evidence to secure a conviction. However, it's possible that information you provide in confidence might be of some assistance so we would certainly encourage you to go to the police and tell them what you know but making clear your unwillingness to be involved in any criminal proceedings.

Q At work, I belong to a pools syndicate of six people and we all pay in £1 a week. There's one girl who is always forgetting to pay and she's even missed a few weeks so we've made up the difference. Last week, we won £30 and she hadn't paid but we still split it six ways. However, thinking ahead hopefully to a bigger prize, we wonder what her legal position would be if we'd made up her stake and then hit the jackpot. Would she be entitled to a sixth of the money?

A If you agree between the five of you to include your sixth member as part of a syndicate then she could well be entitled to claim her share – less her stake money. If, however, you object to her taking advantage of your generosity, you should make it clear *now* that if she does not pay on time, she will be excluded from any money you win.

———

Q I've bought a great leather jacket from one of the maintenance men around the building where I work. I couldn't resist it although I've a deep suspicion that it 'fell off the back of a lorry'. What would my situation be if what I suspect is true and the man were arrested?

A If you purchase an item in circumstances that cause you to know, believe or have a 'deep suspicion' that the item is stolen, then you could well be charged with 'handling stolen goods' if the purchase is traced to you. If it were not for persons prepared to buy goods that had 'fallen off the back of a lorry', the market for thieves would be greatly reduced. That is why handling stolen goods is often regarded as even more serious than theft. So your 'great bargain' might well have its collar felt! (See also pp. 87, 119.)

———

212

Q I love everything about my fiancé. There's just one thing wrong with him. I have a very nice surname and his is horrible. Is it possible for the man to take his wife's name when they marry instead of the other way round?

A Only one thing wrong with him? My goodness, you're a lucky girl! Now, as to that one wrong thing. The adoption by a wife of her husband's name is a long-accepted convention but there is absolutely nothing to stop you turning that convention round and have your husband adopt and be known by your surname. He can call himself what he likes but if he wishes to change his name to yours formally, he can do so by deed poll or, in Scotland, by simply advertising the fact. (See also pp. 4, 68, 69, 70.)

——

Q How do laws get made or changed? Is it the province of the Law Lords or can the Government of the day just change them? If I felt a law should be changed or introduced, could I as a private individual do anything about it?

A For a short answer to your question, we can tell you that laws are constantly changed both in the courts and in Parliament.

In the courts, you sometimes need go only as far as the Court of Appeal to pronounce on a point of principle raised in a case argued before it. When the court appears to change the law, they are in fact declaring that the new interpretation is merely what the law has always been but is now being 'properly' applied: i.e. the law is changed while the court is telling us that this is really what it was all the time (see George Orwell's *1984* for a similar approach).

Parliament, on the other hand, has no such pretence. The

Government of the day, with a working majority, simply issues new statutes or changes old ones as it suits them.

As a private individual, all you can do is petition your local MP and persuade him/her of the need for a legal change. If the MP is high enough in the yearly parliamentary ballot, by which means he can push forward a private members' bill covering your point, you have a glimmer of a chance that your ideas are enshrined into statute.

The only other route open to you is to find yourself embroiled in litigation which raises an important legal issue. You then go on the expensive route to the Court of Appeal or even to the House of Lords and if you win: hey presto, you have created new law (or at least a new interpretation on old law).

That's the short answer! For the long answer, well . . . that's another book!

APPENDIX

There are lots of organizations ready to answer your questions. Your local library should be useful here as well as the citizens' advice bureau or law centre. We list below some helpful addresses.

GENERAL APPLICATION
The Law Society
113 Chancery Lane
London WC2A 1PL
0171 242 1222

The Law Society of Scotland
26–28 Drumsheugh Gardens
Edinburgh EH3 7YR
031 226 7411

The Law Society of Northern
  Ireland
98 Victoria Street
Belfast BT1 3JZ
0232 231614

The National Council for Civil
  Liberties
21 Tabard Street
London SE1 4LA
0171 403 3888

Rights of Women
52–54 Featherstone Street
London EC1Y 8RT
0171 251 6577

Action for Victims of Medical
  Accidents (AVMA)
Bank Chambers
1 London Road
Forest Hill

London SE23 3TP
0181 291 2793

Solicitors Complaints Bureau
Victoria Court
8 Dormer Place
Leamington Spa CV32 5AF
0926 822007/8

Legal Services Ombudsman
22 Oxford Court
Manchester M2 3WQ
061 236 95632

Law Society: Accident Line
(Freephone)
0500 192939

EMPLOYMENT
Central Office of the Industrial
    Tribunal
(*England and Wales*)
100 Southgate Street
Bury St Edmunds
Suffolk IP33 2AQ
0284 762300

Central Office of the Industrial
    Tribunal
(*Scotland*)
St Andrews House
141 West Nile Street
Glasgow G1 2RU
041 331 1601

Advisory Conciliation and
    Arbitration Service (ACAS)
REGIONAL OFFICES:

(*Northern Region*)
Westgate House
Westgate Street
Newcastle on Tyne NE1 1TJ
0632 612191

(*Yorkshire and Humberside
    Region*)
Commerce House
Leeds LS2 8HH
0113 243 1371

(*North Western Region*)
Boulton House
17–21 Chorlton Street
Manchester M1 3HY
061 228 3222

(*London*)
Clifton House
83–117 Euston Road
London NW1 2RB
0171 396 5100

(*South Eastern Region*)
Westminster House
Fleet Road
Fleet
Hants. GU13 8PD
02520 811868

(*South Western Region*)
27A Regent Street
Clifton

Bristol BS8 4HR
0117 974 4066

(*Midlands Region*)
Leonard House
319–323 Bradford Street
Birmingham B5 6ET
021 622 5050

Office of Scotland
Franborough House
123–127 Bothwell Street
Glasgow GR 7VR
041 204 2677

Office for Wales
Phase 1
Ty Glas Road
Llanishen
Cardiff CF4 5PH
0222 762636

Health and Safety Executive
(National Centre)
Baynards House
1 Chepstow Place
Westbourne Grove
London W2 4TF
0171 243 6000

CLAIMS FOR COMPENSATION
FOR CRIMINAL INJURY
Criminal Injuries
Compensation Board
Monley House
Holborn Viaduct
London EC1A 1BP
0171 936 3476

Criminal Injuries
Compensation Board
(*Scotland*)
Blyth Wood Square
200 West Regent Street
Glasgow G2 4SW
041 221 0945

CLAIMS ON ROAD WHERE
DRIVER UNTRACED OR
UNINSURED
Motor Insurers' Bureau (*for
England, Wales and
Scotland*)
152 Silbury Boulevard
Milton Keynes MK9 1NB
0908 240000

HOME BUYING AND
MORTGAGES
Building Societies Association
3 Savile Row
London W1X 1AF
0171 437 655

DIVORCE AND SEPARATION
Marriage Guidance Council
(Relate)
National Headquarters
Little Church Street
Rugby CV1 3AP
0788 573241

Marriage Guidance Council
(Relate)
(*Scotland*)
105 Hanover Street
Edinburgh EH2 1DJ
031 225 5006

Divorce Conciliation and
  Advisory Service
38 Ebury Street
London SW1N 0LU
0171 730 2422

CHILDREN
The Children's Legal Centre
20 Compton Terrace
London N2 2UN
0171 359 6251

Scottish Child Law Centre
1 Melrose Street
Glasgow G4 9BJ
041 333 9305

British Agencies of Adoption
  and Fostering
Skyline House
200 Union Street
London SE1 0LY
0171 593 2000

VIOLENCE OR CRISIS
Rape Crisis Centre
P.O. Box 69
London WC1X 9NJ
0171 837 1600

Women's Aid Federation
(*England*)
National Helpline
52–54 Featherstone Street
London EC1Y 8RT
0272 633542
0171 251 6537

(*Northern Region*)
18 Park Road
Leeds 1
0113 244 4060

STATE BENEFITS OR
INFORMATION
Disability Alliance
Universal House
Wentworth Street
London E1 7SA
0171 247 8776

Age Concern
Astral House
1268 London Road
Norbury
London SW16 4EQ
0181 679 8000

Scottish Council for
  Disablement
5 Shandwick Place
Edinburgh E82 4RG
031 229 8632

DATA INFORMATION ON
CREDIT REFERENCES
CCN Systems Limited
Talbot House
Talbot Street
Nottingham
0115 986 8172

Infolink Limited
Coombe Cross
2/4 South End
Croydon

Surrey CR0 1DL
0181 686 7777

Registry Trust Limited
173–175 Cleveland Street
London W1P 5PE
0171 380 0233

Director General of Fair
    Trading
Field House
Bream's Buildings
London EC4A 1HA
0171 242 2858

INDEX